SAY 'YES' TO LIFE!

THE BOOKS OF MRS. MOW . . .

Your Child

Going Steady With God

Say 'Yes' to Life!

SAY 'YES' TO LIFE!

by
ANNA B. MOW

*Christian growth is a daily saying
'Yes' to Life and 'No' to death*

ZONDERVAN PUBLISHING HOUSE
GRAND RAPIDS, MICHIGAN

To
those who know about being born into new life but are puzzled by their growing pains.

INTRODUCTION

I can think of nothing I could be asked to do which would give me more genuine personal pleasure than to write an introduction to the first book of my beloved friend, Anna Mow. I can also think of nothing which could fill me with more "unearned humility."

Before I speak of her book, I must speak of Anna Mow, the woman.

When I am in a real dilemma, I invariably turn to Anna Mow. I have been doing this throughout much of my sometimes bumpy Christian life. She has never done me the injustice of giving me answers. Instead, I have found her always able to throw open a wide, new door, through which (if I am sincere) I can walk out of my problem in God's energy. More than anyone else, she is responsible for having shown me the altogether important difference between *static* and *dynamic* Christianity.

The fortunate thousands who have heard her speak, in retreats of all kinds across America and in her beloved India, know her as a great human being through whom God has found unique freedom to pour His wisdom and love. People travel hundreds of miles to be relaxed and released as they listen to Anna's clear, direct teaching. More often than not, they find the wonder of the truly free life in Christ simply breaking over their frustrations and heartaches as they sit there listening.

Men stand in pulpits across America more certain of the greatness of God because they were fortunate enough to have sat under the gracious, good-humored, astute teaching of Dr. Mow in seminary. Husbands and wives live together in realistic harmony because one or both have counseled with her. I know of no one whose down-to-earth counseling is more effective with a wider variety of human beings. This is true simply because she sees deeply into both the heart of God and the hearts of people. As when one talks with God, one is unaware of being "counseled" during a talk with her. And one takes her advice because it not only has the rare ring of Holy Spirit authenticity, but it comes mellowed by her spontaneous laugh and her great human tenderness.

Is it any wonder that I hounded her to write this book? Is it any wonder that I am looking forward to its use in the Master's hands with such genuine excitement?

Say 'Yes' to Life! can change your life. On its readable pages you will find a condensate of Anna's own discoveries lived out in a lifetime of service and exploration into the tremendous potential in store for anyone who decides to cooperate with God. More than that, it is the one book I know which can free the bound Christian who honestly doesn't understand why he is bound! Ideas are not set forth in this book and then backed up with Scripture. They are grounded *first* in the Word of God and then developed in a style so simple and readable, one has trouble remembering that Anna Mow is a woman with five degrees after her name. She has trouble remembering this too. She would much prefer that you knew about her twelve grandchildren!

Say 'Yes' to Life! is dynamite to "phariseeism," fresh air to personalities smothered in dogma, nourishment for growth to stunted souls, and a green light to the adventurous ones who dare to follow the big God of the New Testament.

I have not been able to quote from *Say 'Yes' to Life!* because I would simply have to copy the whole book. Everything she writes is quotable. And so I leave the great adventure to you as you begin your own discoveries in its comfortable but provocative pages.

Eugenia Price

Chicago, May 1, 1961

PREFACE

I feel like a child when I say, "Genie made me do it." After all, hadn't I just "retired"? Why use up all my speech ideas in a book? Then I would have to grow more than I had intended on "retirement." I yielded because God said I am not retired from growing.

Continuous growing seems to be the greatest problem sincere Christians have. I've never figured out how we can be so stupid spiritually when in all other phases of life our eyes can see so clearly. Everyone knows how important it is to grow physically and intellectually. Most people know how important it is to grow emotionally, but few accomplish it. So we have a world in which people are matured physically and intellectually, but they are very immature emotionally. They don't know how to grow emotionally, because they do not know how to grow spiritually.

Then the majority of Christians don't seem to know that they can grow spiritually. They seem to think they either are or aren't Christians. This is as inadequate as to say someone is either dead or alive. He may be just born, or in the strength of maturity, or nearly dead, and still be "alive."

For this reason many Christians are bewildered. They stumble over many stones because they do not know that these are stepping stones to higher life. They are frightened by the very winds that come to strengthen their roots. If they think they have *arrived* when they have just become new members in the Family of God, they will surely be retarded children. They will think they are failures every time they find spots on their garments; they will not have the joy of knowing that there is an adequate laundry department in the Household of God; that there are not only adequate facilities for getting clean but for keeping clean. There are always new things to learn in God's Family and so His children can grow to maturity.

Even Bible readers sometimes miss this Good News. The New Testament not only shows us the way to new life in Christ, but even more, it shows us how to grow in that life. Most of the New Testament was written to Christians who had growing problems. In considering this growth in the new life I have imagined what Paul and Peter and others would say if they sat with us in our circle today. And of course, there are the wonderful words of Jesus, as true today as when He said them in Palestine so many years ago. I have tried to quote these words in like circumstances in our day, as they were spoken in that day.

I have quoted, in the main, from the *Berkeley Version* of the Bible. It is very good in translations on passages concerning growth.

Some of my dear friends are of other doctrines and of other faiths. To you I say, I can speak only of what I have seen and heard. I honor your integrity and love you just as dearly. Others may feel that I have not spelled out the doctrine adequately. This is not a doctrinal study. Besides, I trust the work of the Holy Spirit so fully when His work is given a chance by full acceptance, that I am concerned first of all about that commitment of life.

It isn't "pie in the sky" that we want, it is ability to meet our daily problems. We need discernment to know what is of life and what is of death in this crazy, mixed-up world. And we need power to be "new people" and to grow better every day.

When we *say "Yes" to life,* the miracle will begin.

ANNA Mow

Roanoke, Virginia
May, 1961

P.S. My special thanks to Cecil Dowdy for typing and to Genie Price for reading this manuscript. My love to my husband for his help and his patience. A. B. M

CONTENTS

Part I
LIFE BEGINS

*I have come so they may have life
and have it abundantly.*
                    —John 10:10

CHAPTER 1

Behind Your Face

WHEN I WAS A CHILD I didn't like my nose and I didn't like my chin. But my mother didn't seem to mind my face. She always said, "Beauty is as beauty does." However, that was cold comfort to a child who wanted so much to be pretty. I didn't believe her until I went away to school. There I met a girl who was not pretty, either, a fact as plain as her face. To my amazement she was the most loved girl in school, and one of the smartest. We loved her face, too, and I began to forget mine.

I remember, too, about Abraham Lincoln. The story is told that a political enemy called him two-faced. He retorted, "If I had two faces, do you think I would wear this one?" Now the whole world loves the face he wore. My mother was right—at least about Jane and Abe Lincoln.

Beauty culture advertisements say that anyone can be beautiful. No matter what kind of a face nature gave a woman she can do something about it. Even the men who are concerned about looking handsome or rugged can do something about it. Beauty culture thrives on their patronage, too.

When we returned from India our daughter was a junior in high school. Actually, America was a foreign country to her, even though she was "an American citizen born abroad." There were many bewildering pressures upon her. One I did not like was the high school tendency to the use of too much lipstick. One day Lois asked to enroll in a short charm school course. My first thought was, "A missionary daughter!" and "money for that!" But my second thought let her do it, for which I was afterward very grateful. They taught her that beauty is not something to be put on. It must come from within. Whatever is done to the outside must harmonize with the personality within. They told her that make-up which shows defeats itself; that thoughtfulness of others is the foundation of good manners. That course was worth every cent it cost. It also gave a young girl needed security in a new social set-up.

The greatest sin of religious people is to put on a religious face as a mask to cover up a life which is not in harmony with that face. Recently a despairing Christian said to me, "But a Christian must always smile." He did not know that what he put on his face was not a smile, but a woebegone, artificial grin. Our culture has taught us to be gracious no matter how we feel. The specialist concerned with mental health says we must be honest, "Blow your top when you feel like it." When well-mannered people do this they are so ashamed of themselves they are in worse condition than before.

So our real problem is not what we put on the outside, but it is in the make-up of life. How can we have something on the inside that we are not ashamed to expose on the outside?

Intricately involved with the tension between the inside and outside of me is the tension between me and God, and between me and other people. Many say, "There is a veil or barrier between me and God and between me and other people. I cannot break through to them. I am all penned up inside. How can I get rid of these barriers?" Only God can do this for us. We want to find out how He does this, and even more pertinent, can it be done for me?

Usually we think of hypocrites as those who are selfish or evil on the inside, wearing a religious mask on the outside. I found another kind in a friend I met a year after she became a Christian. I supposed her background to be all pagan until I roomed with her at a summer conference. She knew more Bible than half the ministers. When she would inadvertently reveal her love for the Bible or her knowledge of it, she would blush. When I suddenly came upon her reading her Bible she quickly hid it and then blushed because she hid it. One day I said to her, "You are the strangest hypocrite I ever saw. You are a St. Francis on the inside and a pagan on the outside. When you act like this I am going to call you a pagan saint. When St. Francis comes through I will call you St. Francis." For several years her spiritual growth seemed to seesaw in the struggle between her new inner life and her old pagan habits. When God was winning, her letters would be signed, "S. F." When she felt pagan again her letters would be signed, "P. S." But gradually there were all "S. F." signatures. Death overtook her in the prime of life and in the midst of success in her profession. It must have been a joyous occasion to her to meet her Lord without embarrassment and with no veil between them.

The evangelist who won this friend to Christ was often impatient with her because of her inner struggles in the early years of her new life. I had the privilege of knowing her well enough to have the thrill of seeing the new life gradually break through all the exterior pagan habits and reactions. Through her experience, I learned much about the *process* of the working of God's grace as God had a chance to come into her life and then to permeate her whole being.

This process of the working of God's loving grace has been so amazing in Genie Price's life, too. Her spiritual growth has done even more for my faith in a God who is like Jesus Christ than her initial beginning in that new life. I am ashamed to recall the first time I met her. She had been a Christian only two years then. In this first meeting I did not see the new interior. I saw only a face that still had hard lines (not wrinkles) and a manner that was left over from pagan ways of striving for success. When I learned to know how real the new life within her was, I waited with bated breath for the spiritual earthquakes that would likely come to break through all the left-over patterns of the old life.

Then one day the call came. She was in the depth of despair. The new life was no longer real. All seemed lost. She felt like her old pagan self again. I could not be shocked for God was trusting her with a dark hour. How else can one learn to walk in naked faith with a God who never fails us? Now her new faith was really transferred from faith in what God had done in her life to faith in the One who had done it. Her books reach people's hearts because each book has been accompanied by an earthquake or a dark hour, as well as by the still small Voice.

There are still many churches that have "revival meetings." Most Christians are taught how to receive the initial forgiveness of God. An increasing number of churches have membership or confirmation classes to prepare people to *begin* the new life. But all too few realize the need of guidance and loving understanding while the "babe in Christ" learns to eat, to rest, to walk as a Christian. There are plenty of books about growing up physically but too few about the sometimes painful process of growing up spiritually. Some books on spiritual growth discourage rather than encourage the new Christian when he stumbles on his way. The book sounds easy; His way seems hard. This growing Christian does not realize that many of the misunderstood experiences come in the normal process of growing spiritually.

Lest we feel alone in our problems we can take courage from the fact that the Letters of the New Testament were written to Christians who had difficulties in their spiritual growth. To the Galatians the Apostle Paul wrote, "I am amazed that you are so readily moved away from Him, who called you by the grace of Christ, to another gospel" (1:6). "Are you that foolish, that you would now complete with the flesh after beginning with the Spirit?" (3:3). "You were coming along splendidly; who got in your way, so that you do not follow the truth?" (5:7).

Paul's admonition to all Christians is, "Don't stop growing." The secret of his advice is in II Corinthians 3:18: "But we all, as with unveiled face we see the Lord's glory mirrored, are *changed into the same likeness from one degree of glory to another*, derived as it is from the Lord's Spirit."

Paul spoke out of his own experience. Our adventure is to find out how much of this secret is for us also.

FOR FURTHER STUDY TO PREPARE YOURSELF FOR THIS ADVENTURE:

Write —
1. The story of your early experience of God.
2. List ways in which you have grown in your new life.
3. List ways in which you need to grow.
4. What does your family think of you as a Christian?

CHAPTER 2

The Source of Life

THE APOSTLE PAUL TELLS US that there is no need for disparity between the inner life and the outer appearance; the veil may be lifted and we may look on the glory of the Lord. When we do this something always happens. A change begins to come. It is into a growing likeness of our Lord. However, we cannot achieve this in our own strength; the life for this growth is a gift from God. He is the Source of this life.

The Apostle Paul did not know Jesus in the flesh, so he learned to know Him the same way we do. We can take seriously everything he said about being a "new creature." The cry of nearly every person is, "If only I could be a better person!" Paul can show us the way. Any power available to him is available to us also.

Paul wrote the Corinthians, "If any one is in Christ, he is a new creation. The old is gone. Look! the new has come" (II Corinthians 5:17). In the prayer for the Ephesians he says, "I bow my knees before the Father . . . that He may grant you, in keeping with the wealth of His glory, *to be empowered with strength in the inner self by His Spirit;* that through faith the *Christ may dwell in your hearts;* that you may be rooted and grounded in love, so that you may have power to understand fully with all the saints . . . the all-knowledge-surpassing love of Christ; so *you may be filled up to the whole fulness of God"* (Ephesians 3:14-19).

Jesus was talking about this same kind of experience in His conversation with Nicodemus. Although Nicodemus was a devout and educated religious leader, there was still a secret to religious living which eluded him. Jesus was an enigma to him so he came one night to investigate. When Jesus answered his question he was more bewildered than ever: "Unless a person is born from above he cannot see the kingdom of God." Nicodemus was thinking in physical terms, so Jesus said, "Unless one's birth is due to water and Spirit, he cannot enter the kingdom of God. What is born of the flesh is flesh, and what is born of the Spirit is spirit. Do not feel surprised because I tell you, you need to be born from above" (John 3:1-7).

Another day Jesus used another figure of speech in talking about the same thing: "On the final and most important day of the Feast, Jesus stood and called out, Whoever is thirsty, let him come to Me and drink! He who believes in Me . . . streams of water shall flow from his innermost being." John adds, "He said this concerning the Spirit which believers in Him were about to receive. For as yet the Holy Spirit was not yet given, because Jesus was not yet glorified" (John 7:37-39). John's comment is clear that this coming of the Holy Spirit was dated, that the Spirit was coming in a new way, which was not possible before this time. And, of course, John wrote this many years later when he could speak out of his own experience as well as out of the perspective of history.

Throughout the Old Testament times many people had been given the Spirit of God for special occasions and special tasks. The greatest of these were the prophets of God who spoke for God to the people. But the perennial story seemed to be: "My people have committed two evils: they have forsaken Me, the Fountain of living waters, and they have hewn out for themselves cisterns, broken cisterns, which cannot hold water" (Jeremiah 2:13).

I wonder how many of the people gathered in the temple that last day of the Feast thought about these broken cisterns? To them Jesus was saying, "You don't have to depend on broken cisterns for your spiritual water supply. You can have a spring of living water right inside your heart." Such a source of supply would always be available and adequate, no matter how great one's thirst. If Jesus spoke the truth, we may well wonder why so many Christians say they are dry spiritually. Perhaps they haven't heard this good news yet.

There was a woman of Samaria who heard this good news and she believed it. She was shocked into listening, it is true. But Jesus knew the honest desires down under her bad reputation. Jesus knew, as she did, that Jews had no dealings with Samaritans, that good men did not talk to strange women, that "good" men would fear any acquaintance with such a woman who had had five husbands and now lived with a man who was not her husband. Jesus broke all social and religious barriers to reach down to her thirsty heart. He asked her for a drink and so the conversation was opened. Soon Jesus could say to her, "If you knew God's gift and who really asked you, Give Me a drink, you would have requested of Him and He would give you living water. . . . Whoever drinks from this water shall again be thirsty; but whoever drinks the water I shall give him shall not thirst eternally, but the water I shall give him shall become a well of water within him that bubbles up for eternal life" (John 4:7-10). Even such a woman accepted Jesus' offer. No longer did her reputation count against her. The change in her life counted as a witness to God's power and her village neighbors flocked to see and hear Jesus.

This water signifies the Holy Spirit (John 7:39). The symbol is simple, but sometimes it seems that the majority of Christians have only bewilderment concerning the Holy Spirit. Weighty treatises have failed to explain adequately "the Promise of the Father." Rufus Mosely, one of our modern saints, once said, "The story is so simple the wise cannot see it." Paul said, "The worldly-minded person does not accept things of the divine Spirit; to him they are folly and he cannot understand them, because they are estimated from a spiritual standpoint" (I Corinthians 2:14). Only by simple faith and obedience can the door be opened for understanding.

The question still remains, "Why did this special coming of the Spirit happen on the Day of Pentecost and not before?"

The answer is not all clear, but one thing is evident. Since the Holy Spirit is the power of God at work in the world, power could not be entrusted to people who do not know how to use it. The revelation for that use is in the earthly life of Jesus. Paul wrote to the Philippians: "Let this mind be in you, which was also in Christ Jesus, who, though existing in the form of God, did not consider His equality with God something to cling to, but emptied Himself as He took on the form of a servant and became like human beings. So, recognized in looks as a human being, He humbled Himself and lived obediently to the extreme of death; yes, death by the cross" (Philippians 2: 5-8). This is the story in its briefest form, but even the gospels give us little more than thirty days of His most remarkable sojourn in a small country which still exists today.

His humanity seems more of a miracle than His divinity. He had an unerring instinct to do the right. He was tempted in every respect as we are, yet without sinning (Hebrews 4:15). One thing He had settled in His life, He would do only His Father's will. On that He never hesitated. His temptations lay in the area of His human limitations making it necessary to break through the fog of human ways to the clarity of God's will. On the Mount of Temptation the issues were automatically settled when He knew what they were. The tension was then released, hunger returned, and He saw clearly what principles to follow in His earthly ministry.

His greatest witness was in His daily living. His words of teaching were simply the articulation of what He was. His words came according to the need of the occasion or in response to the longing of needy people. He had no notebook of sermon outlines. He was the outline and the sermon. He chose humble men as His special disciples. They lived with Him and learned from Him, as much as they had capacity for. He had compassion upon the multitudes who were like sheep without a shepherd. He healed the sick, raised the dead, fed the hungry, enjoyed His friends, attended special dinners and weddings, restored dignity and hope to prostitutes and other despised people, forgave the sins of sinners, and had strong words for self-centered, proud and unloving religious leaders.

The whole world loves this Jesus. To act "Christian" has the same meaning among religious people of all faiths. A lovely Hindu girl said to me one day, "I can't understand Christians. Jesus was so beautiful and so wise. He never cared for prestige, honor or power. He loved the poor people, and even His enemies. He gave up everything for others." Then after a long pause she added, "Of course, they murdered Him." (This seemed understandable to her for she, too, had suffered for her ideals. She had been a political prisoner for the freedom of her country when only nineteen.)

"Of course, they murdered Him." The signs along the way pointed to the Cross from the very beginning of His ministry. There was no self-interest in Him. There was no compromise in Him. There was no desire to manipulate men to gain the goals of His mission in life. The legally constituted religious leaders of the day soon began to look askance at this "village carpenter" who had none of the "right credentials." Then the months passed and consternation grew. The masses upon whose following these leaders depended for their security and their power were turning with love and devotion to this humble Galilean. They watched Him constantly to catch Him in a fault. They made special note of all miracles performed on Sabbath days. When He said, "The Sabbath was made for man and not man for the Sabbath," they knew He had legal sanction for this but they used it against Him anyway. For the rest they had to hire false witnesses. They were determined to get rid of Him. They stupidly thought they could have their following back if He were out of the way.

The greatest heartache for Jesus must have been that His beloved disciples strove for first place in the coming kingdom, even up to the shadow of the Cross. They didn't understand about His kingdom. They thought He was going to free them from the occupying army of Rome and re-establish the throne of David. Jesus tried to make them understand, but the first time He talked about the Cross, Peter took Him and rebuked Him and said, "Mercy on You, Lord; this must never happen to You!" Then Jesus rebuked Peter for thinking like men think and not like God thinks (Matthew 16:21-23).

The disciples could not believe the Cross could happen. Even the inner circle, Peter, James and John, slept in the Garden while Jesus agonized for a lost world. For Jesus the last corner was turned toward the Cross. There was no more struggling, only suffering.

In his awful bewilderment and because of his great love for Jesus, Peter was in shock and he denied His beloved Master. How could he do it? The early morning crowing of the cock brought him out of shock and as he looked up, the Master turned and looked at him. Those suffering eyes of loving understanding and mercy broke Peter's heart. He went out and wept bitterly. Peter was not sleepy now. His world had come to an end. What could he do now?

And Judas? He connived to force Jesus' hand politically. "This was a time for action, for revolution. Why was Jesus so naive and so slow?" He might as well make some money in the bargain, too! Poor Judas! In his despair at the failure of his scheme he did indeed take too much action. He could not wait through the night. One more night and he might have known the heart-bursting joy of forgiveness.

Proud, selfish religious leaders put Jesus to death in the most shameful way they knew. All of the subtlety and horror of sin was turned loose on Him. No matter what they did to Him they could get nothing but love out of Him, for there was nothing but love in Him — pure, unadulterated love. "Father, forgive them, for they know not what they do," was His prayer for those who sinned against Him. He did not die for Himself. He died for us.

They laid Him in a borrowed tomb and thought a beautiful dream was finished. They did not know that the story was just beginning. Then came the astounding news, THE LORD IS RISEN! The women brought the first news with a special message for Peter. The Lord would not have him feel he was left out (Mark 16:7).

Also that same morning two men were walking wearily about seven miles from Jerusalem along the road to Emmaus. They were discussing the events of the last few days and the unbelievable news of the Resurrection they had heard that morning. A Man joined them. They did not recognize Him. He asked them about their conversation. They still felt sad.

Cleopas answered, "Are you a lone visitor in Jerusalem, so you do not know the late events?" He asked, "What events?" They told Him, "About Jesus of Nazareth, who was a mighty prophet in practice and in preaching before God and all the people, and how the chief priests and our leaders gave him up to be sentenced to death and had him crucified. But we had hopes that he was the one who would deliver Israel" (Luke 24:18-21). They also told the stranger about the morning's report, but did not seem to be able to believe it. The stranger interpreted the Scriptures to them and said, "Did not Christ have to suffer all this so as to enter into His glory?" They did not recognize Him until at their table He blessed the bread. In the prayer their eyes were opened, but they could no longer see Him physically. They said to each other, "Did not our hearts glow within us while He was talking to us on the road?"

They returned to the disciples and others gathered together in Jerusalem and were greeted with the glad news, "The Lord has risen indeed, and has appeared to Simon!" They shared their great experience of the day. While they were telling all this, Jesus was suddenly in their midst. They could not believe their eyes, so He asked for food and they gave Him some broiled fish which He ate. Then He opened their minds to understand the Scriptures and said, "So it is written that Christ should suffer and rise from the dead on the third day, and that repentance, leading to forgiveness of sin, must be preached in His name to all nations. Beginning from Jerusalem you are witnesses of these things, and I will send out upon you the promise of My Father. But you wait here in the city until you are clothed with power from on high" (Luke 24:45-49).

"He then conducted them out as far as by Bethany, and, raising His hands He blessed them. And while blessing them, He was parted from them." They returned to Jerusalem *with great joy* and waited for the promised Holy Spirit.

So Jesus, the Son of God, lived on earth like a man. He was a man. We can look at Him and say, "This is what God is like." At last man can lay aside his misunderstandings about God. God is Love. Even to death Jesus revealed how much God is Love. For a distraught world and despairing church members, the Good News is just beginning. The story of Jesus is a continued story, continued through the work of the Holy Spirit.

DO YOU WANT TO KNOW MORE?

Then read the Gospel according to Mark through in one sitting. Watch Jesus, the Hero of the story. Write down what impresses you about this Man.

Next read the Gospel according to Luke through in one sitting. See what Luke the physician emphasizes about this Man, especially in relation to sinners and neglected people.

Now try Matthew, in one sitting, if you can make it. Take seriously the teachings of Jesus and consider their application in our day.

The Gospel according to John will now break your heart in the portrayal of the suffering of an innocent Man, but your heart will rejoice at the great teachings of Jesus on the Holy Spirit.

The gospels were written to tell the story of Jesus on earth. They are about Him. Read them as if you had never heard the story before.

CHAPTER 3

Life Itself

My SEATMATE ON THE TRAIN was a young girl. She looked like any city teen-ager. I was startled when she interrupted my reading to ask timidly, "Are you saved?" I answered, "Yes, are you?" Wistfully she said, "Yes, but——" and she faltered. I asked what church she belonged to. She told me and then I said, "Your church has two questions. I'll ask you the second one, 'Have you received the baptism of the Holy Spirit?'" Out of the mouth of this city teen-ager came the despairing answer, "No. Every Sunday night the young people in our church go to the altar. We cry and cry for the Holy Spirit, but nothing ever happens. We get so discouraged." So I said, "My dear child, I was not taught to ask either of these questions, but I will tell you from God's Word that you will never receive the gift of the Spirit by weeping. You cry for your sins until they are forgiven, but you open your extended hands with joy and expectancy for the gift Jesus promised you."

(If anyone is going to ask these two questions they should always add a third question, "Are you *growing* in the Spirit?")

When Jesus was in the grave the disciples were without hope. When He disappeared from their sight near Bethany they were full of hope. From the Resurrection to the Ascension they had learned that He was present all the time whether they could see Him or not. He was not dead, He was their Living Lord. Without questioning they believed what He had told them. So they returned to Jerusalem and *waited*. They did not know what would happen. They were not waiting for a "religious experience." They were rejoicing in a Living Lord, they believed what He said, and they continued together in praise and prayer.

As they praised God and waited, the Festival Day of Pentecost arrived. "They were all unitedly in one place, when suddenly there came a roaring from heaven like the driving of a mighty wind and it filled the whole house where they were sitting. There appeared to them also tongues like flames that were distributed and that settled on each one of them. *And they were all filled with the Holy Spirit*" (Acts 2:1-4).

The accompanying phenomena were incidental to the fact of the infilling of the Spirit. Perhaps the most important fact of the phenomena was that the same thing happened to each one present, about one hundred and twenty people, men and women alike. The ones who were not apostles received the same as those who were apostles. This was not just for leaders, it was for all followers of Jesus.

As Peter spoke for all of them he did not glory in their feelings, but he gloried in the Living Lord. Now Peter understood that this was a fulfillment of the prophecy of Joel as well as the fulfillment of the promise Jesus had given them. They had waited and they knew now that this was what they waited for. Jesus was now both Lord and Christ of which fact this day was proof.

The crowds that gathered were deeply moved but they did not acclaim Peter as the coming evangelist of the day. Even the crowds seemed more conscious of God's Presence than of any phenomena they had seen or heard. The Spirit worked in their hearts, too, to conviction. They cried, "Brother men, what should we do?" Peter knew the answer, "Repent and be baptized, each of you in the name of Jesus Christ for the forgiveness of your sins, and *you will receive the gift of the Holy Spirit; for the promise is to you and to your children and to all those far away* as many as the Lord our God may call."

Three thousand souls were added to the Christian fellowship that day. Every one received the gift of the Holy Spirit. The Church, the Body of Christ on earth, was born that day. The

Holy Spirit is still adding to the Church for the promise is to us, too.

If we stop with the second chapter of Acts we will never find out what really happened on that day. The whole book of Acts is the story of what happened. It is the Acts of the Holy Spirit working through the Apostles and all the other new Christians. They had such great fellowship in the Lord that they even sold their possessions and lived as a big family, the Household of God. Their number continued to increase daily.

The *naturalness* with which they brought healing and blessing to others was an astounding change, even from the days when they walked daily with Jesus the Master. "Neither silver nor gold is mine, but I will give you what I have: in the name of Jesus Christ the Nazarene, walk" (Acts 3:6). The lame man walked and praised *God*. This is in sharp contrast to the self-conscious joy of the seventy when they reported to Jesus after their evangelistic tour, "Lord, even the demons are subject to us in Your name" (Luke 10:17). Now there is not so much surprise as expectancy for the power of God to be manifest.

The courage of the Spirit-filled Christians was more than a developed courage. It, too, was part of the gift of the new power. Only a few weeks earlier Peter quailed before a servant girl. Now all sense of fear was gone. In fact, after persecution came, they reported to the brethren and their prayer to God was, "And now, Lord, notice their threats and endow Thy servants with fearlessness to speak Thy word as Thou reachest out Thy hand to heal and to work signs and wonders through the name of Thy holy Servant Jesus" (Acts 4:29). The young church grew in numbers, faith and power until they were accused of turning the world upside down (Acts 17:6).

It is surprising how many things Jesus had to leave unsaid. He did not tell them that the day would come when they should drop the Old Testament ways of worship. They continued in the synagogue and temple worship according to previous custom. But they added their Christian meetings in pri-

vate homes on the first day of the week, for that was the day
of the Resurrection (every Sunday is "Easter"). They gradually
sloughed off old ways as they meant less and less, and the new
ways in Christ filled their lives.

Jesus did not tell them what the new church should do about
the Gentiles. This was their race question. But as they faced
each new issue they were given the discernment to know what
to change and the courage to do it. In fact, Jesus considered
this the work of the Holy Spirit rather than His when He was
with them as a Man. There is a law of readiness in spiritual
growth as there is in other kinds of growth. The disciples were
not ready for these lessons earlier.

Jesus' final teaching on the Holy Spirit was on the night
before He was crucified. He could face their failures then because He knew such failure was to be expected before they
came to Pentecost. There was no secretary that night (John
13-17) to take down the wonderful truths Jesus tried to communicate to them. It is worth even more to know that years
later when every word had been tested by their experience the
words of Jesus could be written down. This is living communication.

The Apostle Paul meant much the same thing when he
wrote to the Corinthians, "In God's presence I have such confidence through Christ, not because we possess self-sufficiency
to form personal judgments; but because our sufficiency is God-
given. And He has qualified us to be ministers of this new
covenant, not of written law, but of a spiritual nature; for the
letter kills, but the Spirit makes alive" (II Corinthians 3:4-6).
Jesus did not expect them to be mere imitators of His ways but
through His Spirit they were to have the mind of Christ to
know what He would do in any situation. This is how the
Spirit was to give life.

We can look back with them to the things Jesus said about
the Holy Spirit before He left them as a Man. "The believer
in Me shall himself do the deeds that I do, and shall do greater
things than these, for I go to the Father, and I will bring about

whatever you ask in My name, so that the Father may be glorified in the Son. I will do whatever you may ask in My name" (John 14:12-14). "I will ask the Father and He will give you another Comforter to stay with you forever, the Spirit of Truth whom the world cannot receive, because it neither observes nor understands Him, for He remains with you and will be within you. I shall not leave you orphans; I will come to you" (John 14:16-18).

Jesus gave the disciples a parable of the Holy Spirit (John 15): "I am the true Vine and My Father is the Tiller. Remain in Me and I in you. Just as the branch cannot bear fruit of itself without staying on the vine, so you cannot without staying in Me. I am the Vine, you are the branches. He who remains in Me — and I in him — bears rich fruit. Apart from Me you can do nothing."

Too many Christians think proximity is enough for their growth and fruitbearing. Peter was close to Jesus for several years, he loved Jesus with all his heart, but mere closeness was not enough in his terrible hour. After the coming of the Spirit Peter had a new power and stability. This was, indeed, a new Peter. For growing, the life must be on the inside. Through the Spirit Jesus is the Way, the Truth, and the Life.

We could use the blood system of our bodies as a parable also. The blood is the life. Blood is repulsive only when one thinks of dead blood. The songs about the blood of Christ fell into disrepute in some circles because people thought of death only, or they thought of blood in the sense of a charm. The blood of Christ is so important because He gave His *life*. There were three crosses on Calvary. Only one was of infinite value because of the life that was given on it. In holy communion we make an important statement: "This cup is the new covenant in My blood. Do this as often as you drink it in remembrance of Me." This should always be an experience of *life*.

In these recent years no one should mind the use of the word blood. In a blood bank drive in Chicago a young woman ran out on the street and cried to passersby, "Blood! Blood! Give your blood to save some life!" She was talking about living blood which could be transported ten thousand miles to save a life. Friends of ours had a boy born with blood which was poison to him. The bad blood was removed and replaced with pure blood. Now the little one lives and is growing beautifully. We need new blood, clean blood. This new blood, the life, is the Holy Spirit by which the life of Christ can be in us.

The blood parable has one other analogy. In our bodies we have both good and bad blood. Half of the blood is "bad" because it is flowing through the body collecting impurities to keep the body well. Then we have the mechanism within us to purify this bad blood and send it out through the body again. The little baby had a chance at life when it received good blood for bad. But it could not have lived without heart and lungs to keep the blood purified and flowing through the body. So being born again is not enough, it is only the beginning of life. Through the same life we grow up in Christ.

The apostles in the book of Acts talked about the Holy Spirit when they thought of this new power in their lives. They knew Jesus on earth and to them their Living Lord was now present through the Holy Spirit. The Apostle Paul did not know Jesus in the flesh, he met Him as the Living Lord on the Damascus road, so when he talked about the new power in his life he talked about the "indwelling Christ" or the "Christ in me." These were not two different teachings but their individual ways of communicating about the same experience of the power of God come to dwell in man to give him new life.

So, it can be *God in me, Christ in me* or the *Spirit in me*. It is God the Creator, the Heavenly Father, as revealed in Jesus Christ living in us through the Holy Spirit. The Holy Spirit is the practical part of the Trinity. God is present with us. His Presence is the Holy Spirit. When He is in us we have new life and power for living. We should not quarrel or be confused by the words anyone uses. The only question is: "Do I have this life and this power?" Paul asked the question the apostles' way when he came to Ephesus, "Did you receive the

Holy Spirit on your becoming believers?" (Acts 19:2). This is the most pertinent question for every believer today.

A young girl expressed it this way: "Jesus came to the door of my heart and knocked. I said, 'Come in, Jesus.' He came in and now He lives in my heart. Not long after He came in there was another knock on the door. This time I said, 'Jesus, You go to the door.' He did and when He opened it Satan was standing there. When Satan saw Jesus, he said, 'Oh, excuse me, I got to the wrong door.'" Didn't Paul say the same when he said, "To be empowered with strength in the inner self by His Spirit; that through faith the Christ may dwell in your hearts"?

Many good people talk about a first blessing and a second blessing. There are differing explanations for conversion, new birth, sanctification, etc., but we will try to stay so simple that no one gets lost in explanations. The absolute essential is to keep one's attention on Christ and be completely committed to Him, then we may have faith in the work of the Holy Spirit that we will receive whatever can come to a human being from God, whether we have a doctrine for it or not. Most people are confused because they start with a doctrine instead of with Christ. We will start with Christ and let the doctrine follow.

For further study:

>Read the whole book of Acts through, in one sitting, if possible. Then you will see the drama of the new community under the power of the Spirit.
>
>Compare Peter in the Acts with Peter in the gospels. See where he is the same and where he is different.
>
>List the things Jesus said about the promised Holy Spirit in John 14-17.
>
>Present your own spiritual needs to the same Living Lord.

CHAPTER 4

Say 'Yes' to Life

In the summer of 1958 a beautiful 22-year-old American girl flew to Ceylon to become a Buddhist nun. She sacrificed her long blonde hair, her comfortable life, her fiance, and her medical studies. She said, "I've been convinced that only through Buddhism can I find true happiness." Referring to her fiance, she said, "He took it badly. I gave him up because I realize that marriage and love are selfish." She thought she had to give up all human love in order to give all to God. She did not know that God's love is not like the bird that pushes the other bird out of the nest. God's love does not push other loves out; it sanctifies human love and sets it in its true perspective. Through Christ love for God and human love are not only compatible, they are one and the same quality of love.

Even Christian young people fall into the same dilemma. One night in Chicago our doorbell rang at eleven-thirty. There stood a young couple with deep apologies for bringing their problems at this time of night. All evening they had been greatly troubled. They both loved God very much. They loved each other so much they were afraid their love for one another would hinder their love for God. Perhaps they should give up all plans for marriage. I knew them well. I said to them, "You foolish children! Your love for each other will give you your definition for your love for God." And it has done just that.

Jesus said, "Seek first His kingdom and His righteousness and all these things will be added on for you" (Matthew 6:33). I have a most gracious friend who once belonged to the cocktail crowd. Several years after she became a "new creature" one of the old frustrated crowd said to her, "Darling, I'd give everything I possess to have eyes that sparkle like yours do now." "That's what it takes, my dear, all you possess," she answered. This giving of everything is not merely giving up something I have, it is giving everything I have to the One I love most, Jesus Christ. Giving to a special One means so much more than giving all to a cause, to an ideal, or even to a religion. A half-interested Christian is no match for any person wholly committed to any cause in the world. But anyone wholly committed to God need never be afraid.

The gratitude of the Apostle Paul is expressed in his whole-hearted devotion: "But everything, that was gain for me, I have considered loss for Christ's sake. And, what is more, I regard everything as waste in comparison to the superb value of knowing Christ Jesus my Lord. For His sake I have given up all things and consider them rubbish, in order to gain Christ" (Philippians 3:7, 8).

The call of Jesus is the same to *all* His followers. There is no maximum or minimum standard of consecration for His disciples. "If anyone wants to come after Me, he must deny himself, take up his cross day by day and follow Me" (Luke 9:23). Following Jesus is a *daily* affair, it is not a call to intermittent following. Church attendance alone will not suffice. Following Jesus is done by *being* a new person who *acts* like Jesus Christ more every day.

The greatest crime a minister can commit against his people is to let them think they can be halfway Christians and get away with it. The church must carry much responsibility for a recent June headline spread across my newspaper: This Year's Class Leaves College With No Causes, No Idols, No Myths, No Heroes, in an Uncertain Era! The challenge of Christ hasn't changed. Our youth insistently ask, "What is the difference, after all, between the 'good people' who go to church and the 'good people' who don't go to church?" In many instances it has been their experience that the non-church-goers are more loving and understanding than the church-goers!

I remember when the majority of Americans felt embarrassed to have religion brought into a daily conversation. Even some ministers made a special point during the week to show that they were jolly good fellows. The American climate has changed. For some years now religion has been popular. Every kind of magazine carries articles on prayer and other religious subjects. Even the Apostle Paul made the cover of *Time* magazine!

Yes, religion has become popular, but, unfortunately, sin is also popular. In fact, sin is so popular that in order to sell perfume they name it *My Sin!* I made this statement at a Youth Retreat last spring. That night when I went to my room in the parsonage I noticed a bottle of perfume on the bureau. I had to look at its name. No, it wasn't *My Sin.* It was worse than that, it was a brand evidently named to attract church members. Believe it or not, the name of it was *Slightly Wicked!* The motivational research advertisers found out about the people who don't want to sin, but they don't want to be fully consecrated, either. Halfway consecration is what they reach for, partly good, slightly wicked!

In 1850 only sixteen per cent of Americans were members of churches. In 1956 over sixty-two per cent were listed as church members. But even with church statistics in the success category, divorce statistics remain disturbingly high, juvenile delinquency is on the increase, mental and nervous breakdowns seem to be on the increase, dope addiction and alcoholism do not decrease, too early marriage, as well as illegitimate babies, are the cause of heartbreaks in too many of our good homes. Evidence of lowered moral fiber is breaking out everywhere, on the air, in the streets, and even in the sanctuary of our homes. Our church membership is now so high that if all members were as serious about Christ as the communists are about their doctrine, many of the evils of our day could be checked in short order.

The church is indeed alert and lively now. Some churches even give out stamps for attendance! The real question is: Is the church alive to Christ? Is the church's vitality more than

that learned in group dynamics laboratories? Are her results
only the expected ones from good publicity agents? Is the
church merely a reflection of today's culture or will the church
be able to influence that culture for needed changes?

The church that developed after the day of Pentecost was
not a club or a memorial society. It had power, it could not be
manipulated, it did not compromise, but with that strength
it had love and mercy. It was so alive it was its own publicity.
Every day brought joy because of the Risen Lord.

How meager our seasonal celebration! Some years ago a
famous restaurant advertised during Lent, "Lent becomes an
enjoyable sacrifice here where fresh fish and the new spring
vegetables are at their best." The businessman can see that we
feel we must sacrifice, but we'd like it to be as comfortable as
possible. It was years before I knew that the Mardi Gras celebration is one last fling of unrestrained pleasure before Lent to
help the poor "faithful" endure the long days of sacrifice until
the feasting of Easter is permitted. On this last Easter Sunday
our paper announced, "Lent's went, now we're pleasure bent."
There are more than years between such celebrating and that
first Easter morn!

One Sunday morning in India a beautifully dressed woman
visited our church. She called in our home the following
Wednesday. We had a normally interesting visit until suddenly
she said, "I have to find where they buried Jesus. He died,
you know." I said, "That was long ago. He did die, but He
did not stay dead. He arose from the grave." She told me of
her long search for His grave. Of course, by this time I knew
she was mentally ill. After she departed it was hard to shake
off the ghostliness of her compulsion. Then I thought to myself, "Well, who is crazy, after all? This poor woman who
imagines such a story or all the people who say they believe
in a living Lord but live as if He were dead?"

We must be more concerned about Christians being "new
creatures" than we are about mere numbers. This is the way
it was in the Jerusalem church, and they had numbers, too.
"Daily the Lord added to the group those who were being saved"

(Acts 2:47). This is no questioning about any method of evangelism, it is only a check on the quality of it. On the bulletin board of an Indiana church for a week was the announcement: REVIVAL. During the last service of the series someone changed the bulletin board to read: REVIVED. When this happens in a church people will come of their own accord, for many of the nonchurch people want God. They simply don't know if they can find Him in the church on the corner.

This "complete commitment" that the preachers talk about is not something nebulous. It is *our part* in the great encounter we have with Jesus Christ. It is a matter of individual choice. God limited Himself in Creation by giving man the right and responsibility of choice. He never overrides a man's will. He *draws* man. "And I, when I am lifted up from the earth, shall *draw* everyone to Myself" (John 12:32). God takes the initiative to call us to Himself. We know this through the Word of God and have found it true from experience. All other religions on this earth teach that the virtue in religion is in the *seeking*, man taking the initiative to find God. For them this becomes a lifelong process of *seeking*. The quality of life at times in some of the world's religious seekers is astounding and challenging. God knows when they are ignorant of His search for them. But we waste energy when we try to do God's part. We need all that energy and discipline to do our own part, which is to *respond. to His prior call.* Our response includes an acceptance of the gift of His Presence which He gives when we choose to be full disciples. I heard Martin Buber, the great Hebrew philosopher, say, "God comes in wherever He is let in." Only through Jesus Christ do we know how much He can be let in. "We love because He first loved us" (I John 4:19). When we truly look to Jesus Christ as Lord we join with Isaac Watts in singing:

> Were the whole realm of nature mine,
> That were an off'ring far too small;
> Love so amazing, so divine,
> Demands my soul, my life, my all.
> (From "When I Survey the Wondrous Cross")

FOR FURTHER STUDY:

Perhaps no chapter in the Bible has more practical advice for the Christian than the twelfth chapter of the Letter to the Romans. Read it through carefully.

Now list each characteristic Paul presents and compare your own life with each.

You need not be discouraged, for He reaches out to you. You need only the discipline of response.

You may find *Testament of Devotion* very helpful (by Thomas Kelly. Harper's).

CHAPTER 5

Say 'No' to Death

SAYING "YES" TO LIFE involves a "No" to the things which lead to death. During the war the girls sang, "You can't say 'No' to a soldier," but from the tragic results they wished they had learned to say, "No." It is even harder to know what to say "no" to in order to truly say "yes" to life. The songs and appeals that press upon us now are more subtle.

"Are you facing difficult problems? Poor health? Money or job troubles? Unhappiness? — Would you like more happiness, success, and good fortune in life? Then learn the new way to pray — " This is from an advertisement in the Sunday magazine section of a large city daily paper. There is nothing wrong with the ad except the underlying inference that I want God for what I can get out of Him.

One day a man gave a little boy a watch. The boy was delighted and he walked down the street admiring his watch. After a while he came opposite the town clock. He compared the time with his little watch. The town clock was wrong! So he got a ladder, climbed it and set the town clock to match his little watch. This is only a story, but it is a parable of our wills and God's. *His* is the way that is right for us.

It seems easy in a high moment to decide to follow Christ all the way. Then come bewildering failures which throw us into darkness unless we know what to expect and what to do. There is a discipline of commitment, for there is no choice unless the choice is followed by action. The choice must now be related to every phase of life.

Responsibility in relation to choice is often hard to learn. The

first important consideration is in making the choice. Careful
thought is the mature way. Even Jesus asked people to consider the cost before they decided to follow Him. Making a
choice for Christ is much like making a choice in marriage.
When mature people take marriage vows seriously, after they
have carefully chosen one another, they are prepared to stay
together no matter what happens. They have settled one thing,
they will stay together. So when the way becomes difficult, as
it likely will at times, they have only to find the way through
the difficult hour.

Immature people make choices hastily and without thought,
in marriage and for Christ. The choice may even be right, and
the problem be one of immaturity only. If this be true, it helps
to recognize it. I know a woman who could never make up her
mind about her choice of clothes. One time she bought a dress
and exchanged it seven times before she kept one. And the
last one she kept was the first one she had brought home! The
"doctrine of backsliding" is made for those who cannot decide
what they want and cannot abide by any choice. They are the
dear folks who have to be reconverted at every annual revival
meeting. They never get out of the nursery in the Household
of God.

After careful consideration a mature person makes a decision
with the assurance that it is worth staying by it. Of all choices,
the one to follow Christ is the wisest. The only hitch is in
putting this choice into daily living. It is easier to say "Yes"
to Christ who is life, than it is to recognize the "no" involved
to maintain the "yes." So-called popular religion gets lost in
this fog. The crux of the whole problem is *"self."* Jesus said,
"If anyone wants to come after Me, he must deny himself, take
up his cross day by day and follow Me, for whoever wants to
save his life shall lose it, but whoever loses his life on My account, he will save it" (Luke 9:23, 24). The big "Yes" is to
Christ and the big "No" is to self. We shall see that getting
rid of self is not as frightening as it sounds.

The ad men who thought Christians wanted an easy sacrifice during Lent did not understand the cost of sacrifice, but they did unintentionally speak a real truth: It is an "enjoyable sacrifice." Just look what we get for what we give up. In fact, in comparison it does not seem like a sacrifice at all. We marvel at the sacrifices David Livingstone made, yet he himself said, that in his whole life he never made a sacrifice.

One of the most unusual stories from the early ministry of Jesus is the seeming ease with which His disciples left their jobs to follow Him. And this was in a land where the son followed in the father's occupation. It could not be that they were irresponsible, restless men who followed anyone who came along. The reason must have been in the dynamic appeal of the Man Jesus. There was something in Him that made them want to leave everything to follow Him.

Paul felt the same way when called by the Risen Lord, "But everything, that was gain for me, I have considered loss for Christ's sake. And what is more, I regard everything as waste in comparison to the superb value of knowing Christ Jesus my Lord. For His sake I have given up all things and consider them rubbish, in order to gain Christ and to be found in Him" (Philippians 3:7, 8).

So often the more we try to give up self, the more firmly it seems to be established. One young man cried out, "I can't get rid of self unless I commit suicide. I deny myself, but every morning when I wake up I am still here." Too often, when we are told we must give up self if we want to have Christ, the appeal is "Surrender! Surrender!" without adequate emphasis on the *One* to whom we surrender. We get all tangled up in the verb and forget the object of the verb. (We can call this spiritual grammar!)

We have a dear friend in India who was a British-educated Brahman. During his years in England the church made no impression on him. After his return to his homeland an experience came to him which shook his life. He had to find God. He did the only thing he knew to do. He made arrangements for his family as if he were to die, divested himself of everything but the clothes on his back, and without money went out to seek for God. For thirteen years he sought — without finding. He was honest in his search and as the sacrificial years passed he realized he had no success in finding God or in conquering self. The despair of his heart was in his cry, "I am all undone! I am nothing!" But his fellow monks thought this was progress and they said, "You are the holiest of us all." This was more frustrating than ever.

Finally this searching Brahman came across a stray portion of the New Testament, the book of Matthew, which he read for the first time. It spoke to his soul and he wanted to know more. The first Christians he found saw only his outward "holy man" appearance and feared to lend him their books. Then he was sent as a priest to a sacred Hindu city. He thought he was losing all chance of finding more about Jesus, but his real opportunity was just coming. There was a Christian hospital in that city and a Christian church. The Christians there knew there could be a real desire for God in any man's heart, no matter what his outward appearance was. He did find Christ there, the Christ who was seeking him all the time. His family joined him and together they serve in the pastorate of the little church there. Persecutions are incidental to him, for he has so much in Christ.

Jesus threw the whole emphasis on following Him, the giving up of self was incidental to that. As long as one's attention is on self it is an excruciating experience to get rid of it. Only in contrast is the pain mitigated or the process possible. Jesus said the same truth in another way, "I have come so they may have life and have it abundantly" (John 10:10). His emphasis is on *life, abundant life*. The Buddhist says, "Get rid of *all* emotion, the good as well as the bad." But all New Testament teaching to growing Christians says, "Get rid of the bad emotions and be free to develop the good ones."

To the Colossians Paul wrote, "If then, you have been raised with Christ, seek for things above . . . for you have died, and your life is with Christ hidden in God. . . . Deaden, therefore, your organs that tend earthward — unchastity, impurity, passion, evil desire, and greediness, which is idolatry. . . . At one time you were addicted to them, when your life was spent in such ways. But now you must also put all these things away: anger, bad temper, malice, slander, shameful language. Do not lie to one another. Having stripped off the old nature with its practices, and having put on the new self that is being renewed to have knowledge in the likeness of Him who created it, you are where . . . Christ is all and in all. Therefore, as God's chosen, set apart and enjoying His love, clothe yourselves with tenderness of heart, kindliness, humble-mindedness, gentleness, patient endurance. Bear with one another and forgive each other in case one feels a grievance against another. Just as Christ has forgiven you, so do you. But cap it all with love. . . . Let the enriching message of Christ have ample room in your lives. . . . And whatever you may do by word or deed, do it all in the name of the Lord Jesus" (Colossians 3:1-17).

And to the Ephesians: "You must no longer behave like the Gentiles, whose lives are spent in the uselessness of their ways of thinking. You are to rid yourself of the old nature with your previous habits, be renewed in your mental attitude, put on the new nature that is created in God's likeness in genuine righteousness and holiness" (Ephesians 4:22-24).

To the Galatians: "Behave in a spiritual manner; then you will not carry out your fleshly cravings. Now the works of the flesh are in evidence, such as adultery, unchastity, impurity, lewdness, idolatry, magic, animosities, hatred, jealousy, bad temper, dissension, a factional spirit, heresies, envy, drunkenness, carousings and everything of the kind. But the Spirit's fruition is love, joy, peace, an even temper, kindness, goodness, fidelity, gentleness, self-control. There is no law against these. Now those who belong to Christ have crucified the flesh with its passions and desires. If we live by the Spirit, let us also be directed by the Spirit" (Galatians 5:16-26).

In these Letters to the early Christians the contrast between an old life and a new life is very marked. Put off the dirty clothes of the old way of living, be dead to the lower nature, and to this world, put all the old ways behind you, crucify the old nature. Put on clean, fresh clothes, for you have new life, a new holiness which is no illusion. The new life is in the Spirit, in Christ, guided by the Spirit, and the fruits of the new life are from the Spirit.

The old nature must die so that *the new nature may be alive to Christ.*

impurity of mind	purity of mind
evil desires, sexual immorality	fidelity
uncontrolled passion drunkenness	self-control
greed	generosity
evil thoughts, gossip	kindness of heart
bad temper	patience
lies	truth, honesty, integrity
envy, hatred	love, forgiveness
quarrelling, factions	peace, understanding
rivalry, jealousy	humility

These lists sound much like a psychologist's description of an *unhealthy self* and a *healthy self.* Dr. Fritz Kunkel spoke about the *seeming self* which smothered the *real self* so that the real self could not grow. Dr. Karen Horney wrote about the *neurotic self* with its claims, its search for glory, its self-hate and self-contempt, its perverted pride and the binding tyranny of its "should." On the other hand she said, "The real self is the alive, unique, personal center of ourselves; the only part that can, and wants to grow" (*Neurosis and Human Growth*, W. W. Norton & Co., p. 155). Jesus is saying to us, "If any man would come after Me, let him *deny his neurotic self* and follow Me, for I have come that your *real self may have life* and have it abundantly."

Years after Jesus called the disciples, the witness to this possibility was given in the second Letter of Peter: "For His divine power has bestowed on us every requisite for life and godliness, through knowing Him who called us to His own glory and virtue. Through these there have been granted us great and precious promised blessings, so that by means of them you might become sharers of the divine nature, having escaped from the corruption in the world.

"For this very reason, do your utmost to *supplement your faith* with virtue, your virtue with knowledge, your knowledge with self-control, your self-control with patience, your patience with piety, your piety with brotherly affection, and your brotherly affection with love. For if you possess these qualities *increasingly*, they will render your knowledge of our Lord Jesus Christ neither inactive or unproductive, while he, who is not furnished with these, is blind, short-visioned, oblivious of the cleansing from his former sins. Exert yourselves the more then, for *if you practice these things you will never stumble at all*" (II Peter 1:3-10).

The discipline of full commitment to Christ is a daily saying "Yes" to life and "No" to death, without any hesitation whatever.

FOR FURTHER STUDY:

Read the Letters to the Colossians and to the Galatians, and make note of the contrasts between the old life and the new life. List and discuss these in relation to your own experience. Reaffirm your own commitment to Christ in very definite terms.

CHAPTER 6

Testing! Testing!

COMMITMENT TO CHRIST is spontaneous when our attention is wholly upon Him as it is in a high and holy hour of worship. The laboratory, however, for this new life is in the world around us. It is first of all in the home, then in any other close relationships in which we are involved in our daily living. No matter how difficult the problem, how unhappy the situation, a Christlike way must be found to meet it. This way may not always be easy. Jesus went on to the Cross because that was the only way God could reveal His great love to the world. As He revealed the Father we must live to reveal His life and love.

Several months ago I was greatly burdened for a friend who faced a seemingly hopeless situation. I knew she had gone to a Spiritual Life Retreat. I hoped she could see her situation as Christ saw it, whatever that was. I still feel the touch of God's hand of love as I think of her letter: "What did God do for me at the Retreat? I went asking Him for courage to get out of this heartbreaking mess. I argued with God because I wanted out. I spent much time in the Prayer Room, always asking for courage to leave. I finally knew He wanted to give me more than courage to leave, He wanted to give me courage and strength to stay. I was assured that His grace is sufficient if I put self aside. To accept God's grace makes me feel good; to appropriate it makes me want to make others feel good. I find His grace is not full without both—acceptance and appropriation. God has been so good to me I could not bolt this offer from Him."

In reading the Letter to the Ephesians, one's mind and spirit are stretched by the magnitude of the great thoughts presented: Jesus as the center and culmination of history; the power of God available to us for any situation in individual or group experience; the Christ who dwells in our hearts and also is the head of the church which is His body on earth.

One feels overawed with religious joy with these wonderful thoughts until the finger of the Spirit hunts around for sore spots to see if we really are appropriating what He offers to us. "Woman, how do you relate to your husband?" "Man, how do you love your wife?" "Parents, are you carrying your responsibility in training your children so they are capable of knowing God?" "Children, do you obey your parents in the Lord?" "Servants and masters, what is your relationship to one another?" (Management and labor, is your relationship in harmony with your worship on Sunday?)

The general principle to apply to all these relationships is stated in Ephesians 5:21 — "Be submissive to one another out of reverence for Christ." I have just seen a woman who walks in this kind of reverence. She was my hostess for several days. She seemed to have an inner holy quiet which reached out to everyone. It did not separate her from others. It made her available. Interruptions didn't bother her. It was hard to believe that she was once a frustrated woman full of anxiety. Now she goes through the frustrations of the day remembering her Lord whom she represents to everyone who crosses her path. With all this she has a keen sense of humor and a sweet dignity.

"Being submissive to one another" is an attitude usually disdained by Christians as it is by others. Much less is it ever considered any kind of a spiritual law. If we really understood the power of Christ's life we would be less afraid of this idea which is the basic principle of love.

Paul was talking about the same thing when he wrote to the Philippians who were having some troubles among themselves: "If, therefore, in relationship with Christ there is any encouragement, if there is any persuasive appeal of love, if there is any fellowship in the Spirit, if any deep-felt affections and sympathies, then make my joy complete by your mutual identity of purpose, your common object of love, your fellowship of feeling and your harmonious thinking. You will not act from factional motives or out of vanity, but with humble-mindedness each will regard the other superior to himself; neither will each be looking out only for his own interests, but also for those of others.

"Let this mind be in you, which was also in Christ Jesus, who, though existing in the form of God, did not consider His equality with God something to cling to, but emptied Himself as He took on the form of a servant and became like human beings. So, recognized in looks as a human being, He humbled Himself and lived obediently to the extreme of death; yes, death by the cross" (Philippians 2:1-8).

We are inclined to shy away and say, "Yes, but that was Jesus." We who follow Jesus must face the fact of the life of Mahatma Gandhi. He took the law of love and humble service seriously. He submitted himself completely to the welfare of his nation as well as to the lowliest of those he met. He paid no attention to those who told him this way of love would not work in a world like this. It did work and his nation won her freedom. When Gandhi died, humanity lowered its flag. Senator Vandenberg said, "Gandhi made humility and truth more powerful than empires." We said this even more about Jesus but we didn't really believe it.

This spiritual law of selflessness is the key to the entrance of the kingdom of heaven: "Blessed are they who sense spiritual poverty, for theirs is the kingdom of heaven" (Matthew 5:3,5). This is the way this spiritual law is stated in its relationship to God. But in relation to people the same quality of life is called *meekness or gentleness.* "Blessed are the gentle (the meek) for they shall inherit the earth." The world insistently misinterprets meekness and gentleness. It is never weakness, it is always strength. Some who know call them "The Terrible Meek." It is a strength that physical power cannot fathom or threaten.

It is not to be passive, to be pushed around, to cringe in fear. One good look at Jesus should correct that error. Jesus was crucified, but He was never pushed around. He was crowned with thorns, but He was not browbeaten. He never cringed, He never lost His dignity, He was never frightened. Pilate, the governor of the state, with all his military power, was the frightened one. And history says that Jesus was not tried before Pilate, but Pilate was on trial before Jesus.

Some years ago on the first day of a summer retreat a handsome Negro minister rose to tell his greatest need. His head hung low as he said haltingly, "I am a broken man. I have no courage to go on. Even among ministers of the Gospel I don't know whether to be conscious of Christ or of my color." For two weeks he shared fully in a fellowship in Christ. On the last day he stood up with his head held high and said, "I am a new man in Christ Jesus. I can go out from this place and take anything that can happen to me."

On the first day this brother felt humiliated but he was not humble. On the last day when he held his head high with the dignity any man can have in Christ Jesus, he was truly humble, for now he was no longer thinking of himself. Such are the poor in spirit, rich in His Spirit. Such are the meek, strong with gracious dignity because their security is in that which cannot be hurt or shaken.

This is the quality of "being submissive to one another out of reverence for Christ." The Apostle Paul saw this loving submission to the welfare of another as the outstanding characteristic of motherhood. When his heart was broken over the Galatian Christians who so quickly changed their allegiance from Christ to another gospel he cried out to them, "My children, over whom I once more suffer birthpains until Christ is formed within you" (Galatians 4:19). Only in terms of selfless creative motherhood could he express his concern.

Paul took it for granted that mothers would understand what he was trying to say about a quality of life in Christ which would be evident in every relationship. So he said to the women first as wives, "Wives, be submissive to your husbands as to the Lord." This has nothing to do with being a "doormat." It has nothing to do with unwilling or rebellious submission to an intolerable situation. There is no room for self pity because all the energies of a giving love are turned creatively toward the highest well-being of the loved one. This love has courage, patience, hope because of a knowledge of Christ's power available for appropriation in any need.

Those who do not know the power of this giving love are possessed by the great American fear of being "walked over," "henpecked," or being made a "doormat." We have such a fear of the word "obey" that we have unconscious fears of obeying God. This is a fear born from self-interest. Self-interest breeds the very results that it is guarding against. It short circuits real love every time.

Many people do not know that there is a *giving love*. A movie star divorced her fourth husband with this explanation for her numerous marriages: "Four marriages make me seem much worse than I am but that's because I married every man I fell in love with. Love is great. So are men. It's marriage I'm a little disappointed in." (She recently divorced her fifth!)

Real love is not getting, but giving. With reverence I remember a precious little woman who through the years caused me to marvel at her courage in a difficult situation. Her husband is naturally kind and generous, but when drunk he is cruel. She learned to keep quiet, to avoid the things which irritated. She endured because she loved him dearly in spite of his weakness. She also remembered his childhood and adult experiences with unloving church members which caused him to shy away from the church. She knew about his deep spiritual longings. So she has waited with patience. At last, the waiting is bringing results. She has no more need to fear her husband. Recently she said to me, "I consider my marriage a success; I have made my husband happy."

Mothers and wives have no corner on this love market. Giving love is for husbands, too. Some years ago my brother was waiting to become a grandfather. He had almost lost his wife when their daughter Harriett was born. Now Harriett was to have her first child and two weeks had passed since the designated date for the birth. I found my brother pacing the floor. I came up behind him and said, "William, I found it much more difficult to become a grandmother than to become a mother." William answered, "Yes, that's when a woman finds out what a man goes through."

The fact is that Paul wrote more in the fifth chapter of Ephesians for the husbands than for the wives: "Husbands, love your wives, even as Christ loved the Church and gave Himself for her." I speak for all women when I say that any woman would be willing to be a doormat for a man who loved her like that!

It must be understood that this kind of love does not mean *domination* of either one over the other. One man said, "My wife and I are one. I'm the one." In many cases the wife is the guilty one. For a man or a woman to dominate or succumb is an entirely different matter from the healthy chosen submission to another that Paul discusses. The Christian admonition cannot mean domination because Christ never dominates anyone. He *draws* us with His great love.

"Perfect love casts out fear" so neither one feels compelled to protect himself from the other. With such Christ-love in the human relationship even competition becomes irrelevant. We become competitive when we feel our own personalities being threatened by another. The competitive spirit is melted away by giving love. Only through giving love can there be fulfillment in this closest of human relationships.

Two can become one only through this giving love. For those who find this kind of love, life has a great surprise package: the individual personality is not obliterated. Each has a new freedom to be himself. The freedom for fulfillment found in the commitment to Christ is now accentuated in the closest human relationship.

Historically, there is only one thing wrong with "Wives,

obey your husbands." Husbands have used this order on their wives. This admonition is for the wives, and they must *choose* it or it has no spiritual value or power. The admonition for the husbands is, "Love your wife as Christ loved the church." Each to his own personal admonition.

However, the husband is the head of the wife "as Christ is the head of the church." Obviously this does not mean that he can *demand* this headship on "scriptural grounds" even though it has been quoted thus through long years of church history. The clue to the significance of this *headship* I found in a report of a conference on Christian marriage which was held in Woudschouten by the Dutch Reformed Church in July, 1952. They asked the next question which I stupidly didn't think of doing before: "How is Christ the head of the Church?"

The answer to that question is quite clear: "Whoever among you wants to be great must be your minister and whoever would be first shall be your servant; just as the Son of Man did not come to be served but to serve, and to give His life a ransom for many" (Matthew 20:26-28). Christ is the head of the church by being the servant of the church. Therefore, if the husband is the head of his wife as Christ is the head of the church, *he is the servant* of his wife *as Christ is the servant* of the church.

So everyone who loves is a servant. The circle is complete. In Christ's life-giving, serving love for us we have the real definition of the spiritual law for human relationships: "Be submissive to one another out of reverence for Christ."

For further study:

> Compare other references to Christian home relationships.
> I Corinthians 7
> Colossians 3:18-25
> I Peter 2:18 - 3:7

Use your home as a laboratory for testing out "giving love."

CHAPTER 7

Life Means Growth

THE HOME IS NOT THE ONLY LABORATORY in which we test out the spiritual laws of God. All of life is a schoolroom. The real question is, are we learning?

The early Christians had the same life problem of learning. In the Letter to the Hebrew Christians (Hebrews 5:11-14), the writer expresses his concern for them: "While by this time you ought to be teachers, you stand again in need of someone to teach you the elementary beginnings of God's lessons; you have come to need milk and not solid food. Of course, anyone who feeds on milk is inexperienced in the doctrine of being righteous, for he is an infant. But solid food is for the *mature,* for *those whose faculties have been trained by practice to distinguish between good and evil.*"

The Christian who appropriates the grace of God in every circumstance finds himself changing "from one degree of glory to another." Of course, he will not be as conscious of this growth as those who live with him. Some people do not grow more because they do not know they are supposed to grow spiritually, or because they are afraid to change.

We expect a baby to grow no matter how much we adore him as he is. We expect young people to grow, rejoicing that the present stage is not permanent. Then we turn stupid when it comes to spiritual things. We talk about the "new birth" and expect the "babe in Christ" to be finished as soon as he is born. Many evangelists are wonderful spiritual midwives with great skill in helping seekers into the new birth. But even they sometimes become impatient when the "babe" stumbles as he tries to walk. No wonder new Christians become bewildered and discouraged. Instead of receiving help in their growth problems, they are often made to feel guilty because they still have problems.

There is a law of readiness spiritually just as truly as there is physically and intellectually. When my babies were small, the books told us to "train them early." Tiny potties were available for even the three-month-old babies. By the time the little bodies were capable of self-control the little folk were so disgusted with the whole process that diapers had to be used until they were worn out on one baby. Now the little potties are sold in gift catalogues for table decoration and larger ones are available in little chairs, to the delight of the little one now old enough to understand what it is all about. My grandchildren run around in "training panties" and do very well, for they weren't pushed beyond the little body's development.

One of the most remarkable things in a baby is its inward propulsion to grow. Our first baby was the first grandchild on both sides of the family and we were ten thousand miles away from all the grandparents. Every month we took pictures of what Lois had learned to do that month. There is a picture when she first put her toe in her mouth, then of sitting up, standing by a chair, crawling, and walking. These were all major events of her first year. There was always this miracle of an inner propulsion to do the next thing.

The law of readiness and this desire to grow are just as true for the "babe in Christ." Because this is not recognized the new Christian is not properly nourished, encouraged, or understood. If not helped in his first desires to read the Bible, to pray, to serve, he may turn out to be spiritually retarded. Even at "ten" he may not be able to feed himself, to walk, to talk (communication with God), and he may be entirely dependent on others for courage and faith. And so he remains in the spiritual nursery of the church, which is already overcrowded with all the others who never got beyond it.

The Apostle Paul realized the necessity for growth in his

own life. He never rested on his initial experience of Christ, nor did he ever rest on the fact that God used him so greatly. He said, "Not that I have already gotten hold of or already have reached perfection, but I am pressing onward in hopes of laying hold, because I have been laid hold on by Christ Jesus. Brothers, I do not infer that I myself have laid hold; but one thing I do: forgetting what is behind and reaching out for what lies before, I push on to the goal for the prize of God's heavenly call in Christ Jesus" (Philippians 3:12-14).

When Paul talks about what he has not attained we might miss his point if we forget what he has already received by faith through the grace of God: "I am crucified jointly with Christ; I no longer live as I, but Christ lives within me. So, the life I now live in the flesh I live by the faith of the Son of God, who has loved me and gave Himself up for me" (Galatians 2:20). What Paul had attained was the "indwelling Christ" who came not by Paul's effort, but by his commitment in faith. This indwelling Christ which is the Holy Spirit was now the *growing principle* in Paul's life. Perfection was working in his life, but the work of God's grace was not yet perfected. He was still growing. Paul reached out and pushed on toward the goal which was maturity in Christ.

The musician and the athlete can understand what Paul means by such serious discipline toward a goal. They know there is no freedom without consistent discipline. The discipline is in keeping the goal in mind and in growing toward the goal. For Paul it meant that no matter what happened he. was never turned off his course. He never hesitated any time just because the way was hard. He said, "This treasure, however, we possess within utensils of mere clay — an evidence that the unparalleled power is of God and not from us. We are hedged in from every side, but we live no cramped lives; we suffer embarrassments but we do not despair; we are persecuted but not deserted; struck down but not destroyed; all the while bearing about in the body the death marks of Jesus, so that by our bodies the life of Jesus may also be shown" (II Corinthians 4:7-9).

We must learn, as Paul did, that Christian discipline is not a "straining every nerve" to *attain* goodness, to *attain* to the Presence of God, to *become* more spiritual by one's own efforts. Of ourselves we cannot attain these things. Christian discipline always *presupposes grace* and the prior initiative of God's love. This is a discipline which does not have to *seek* God's favor, but which is a *response to God's love*. The demand of love is far more binding than the demand of an "ought." Just as discipline and disciple come from the same root word, so are they one in life; there is no discipleship without discipline.

The "tyranny of the should" and "compulsive obedience" belong to the disciplines followed in order to attain goodness. The disciplines which follow grace lead to freedom. The Galatians broke Paul's heart because they turned away from this freedom in Christ and returned to the slavery of compulsive religious forms. "For this freedom Christ has liberated us. Stand firm, then, and be not held fast again by a yoke of servitude" (Galatians 5:1).

The Galatians had transferred their allegiance from Christ as the goal to the ways of the law, and they thus put themselves outside the realm of grace. Now the emphasis was on doctrine rather than relationship. When this happens love slips away. This makes Christian growth impossible.

Paul said he was living his present earthly life by faith in the Son of God. Maturing comes in the daily growing by this faith. The process or training is in the continuous choosing of the right from the wrong. By practice, skill develops. The spiritual senses become sensitized to the thinking of God. As we look to Him we can trust Him to show us what the next lesson is to be. To the Philippians Paul added, "Let those then who are mature, have this in mind, and if your views differ in any respect, God will make this clear also to you. However, when we have arrived, let us keep moving in the same direction" (Philippians 3:15, 16). Each lesson we learn becomes background for the next lesson. God promises to show us the lessons we still need to learn.

Spiritual learning is much like learning in school. My interests do not turn to mathematics, but I remember how happy I would feel when one section of the subject would finally become clear to me. Then it looked so easy and I wondered why I had not understood it before. It would have been nice to stay there where it wasn't hard anymore, but I always had to move on to another chapter of incomprehensible problems and work hard until they were understandable. Only by this process, however, could I go on to the end of the course. Even so, in life we progress as we tackle new problems.

At intervals examinations come to reveal how well we are doing and to show us what we have still to learn. Dark hours and difficult tasks are life's examination hours. Paul wrote to the Corinthians: "Test yourselves, whether you are in the faith; give yourselves an examination. And this is the object of our prayer — your all-rounded completeness" (II Corinthians 13: 5, 9).

Paul asked for examination before the communion service also. "But let a person have a self-examination" (I Corinthians 11:27-30). Those who do not take time for this examination are likely to eat unworthily and so become sick Christians. Spiritual examination is always done in the light of Christ's love. He does not condemn, He forgives. This is why there is condemnation without this examination. His love has not had a chance. This kind of a self-examination leads one to be more conscious of Christ than of one's self, therefore real communion becomes possible.

There are other hours when life's lessons seem too hard and we find ourselves shrinking back, not realizing that such shrinking back is turning from life and growth, to death. Paul always pressed on toward life. Jesus knew it would be hard for us, but He encouraged the decision for life: "Enter through the narrow gate; for wide is the gate and spacious the road that leads on to destruction and many are those entering through it. Because narrow is the gate and contracted (hard) *the road that leads on to life* and few are its discoverers" (Matthew 7: 13, 14).

We have a choice, always, for life or against it. Jesus is the Way, the Truth, the Life. But we must make the big choice and apply that choice daily as long as we live. We cannot drift into life. Drifting leads through the wide gate to destruction of personality and of life. Each time we reaffirm our basic life choice for the Christ life we grow some more and enlarge the space in our lives for the Spirit to occupy.

"So then, encircled as we are with such a great cloud of witnesses all about us, *let us get rid of every impediment and our besetting sin,* and *let us run steadily the course* mapped out for us, with our eyes on Jesus, the Cause and Completer of our faith who, in view of the joy that lay ahead for Him, submitted to the cross, thought little of the shame, and is seated at the right hand of the throne of God. Compare your experience with His, who was willing to stand so much contradicting from the sinners against Himself, so that your souls may not wear out with despondency.

"My son, do not think lightly of the Lord's discipline, neither feel fainthearted under His reproof; for the Lord disciplines the person He loves. God is testing you as sons. He does it for our benefit, so we may share in His holiness. Of course, all discipline seems at the time not enjoyable but painful; later on, however, it affords those schooled in it the peaceful fruitage of an upright life.

"So, straighten out your listless hands and your shaky knees; step out straight ahead with your feet, so that lame legs may not be dislocated but rather grow healthy" (Hebrews 12:1-13).

It is not what happens to us, but the spirit in which we take what happens to us that determines whether we are set toward life and growth or not.

Do you want to grow more?

> How long have you been a Christian?
> Have you developed spiritually as much as you have intellectually?

What grade are you in God's school?
Make a list of the lessons you have learned.
How many lessons do you have to learn over?
As you know now, what lessons are unlearned?

Jesus is the great Teacher. He says, "Learn of Me."
He is the Life and our growing power.
Do not be afraid. Press on. He waits in love.

Part II
LIFE MATURES

But the Spirit's fruition is
love
joy
peace
an even temper
kindness
goodness
fidelity
gentleness
self-control
There is no law against these.
—Galatians 5:22, 23

For if you possess these qualities
increasingly, they will render your
knowledge of our Lord Jesus Christ
neither inactive nor unproductive.
—II Peter 1:8

CHAPTER 8

Love

THE WORLD'S MAIN PROBLEMS are not scientific. We are doing very well in that area. The real problems are in human relations. Our fears are not really of bombs, but of men who might explode them in sudden anger or thoughtless retaliation. It is fear that drives us and enslaves us. It is fear we must conquer. Nuclear weapons cannot bring this victory. When every great nation has such weapons we are back again to the men who might use them. Our enemy is fear. Do we believe the Word: "Perfect love expels fear"?

When we do not have love we substitute force, in national relations and in personal relations. Even Napoleon Bonaparte saw this contrast: "Alexander, Caesar, Charlemagne, and myself have founded empires; but upon what do these creations of our genius depend? Upon force. Jesus alone founded His empire upon love: and to this very day millions would die for Him."

When Jawaharlal Nehru did not fill the headlines with vituperative language in India's border troubles with China, many Americans took it for granted he was doing nothing about it. (They did not know the legacy from Gandhiji: "Maintain or create a climate of peace so that negotiations for peace are always possible.") The irony of our American humor! They cartooned Nehru, a Hindu, with one cheek already bloody, and the other cheek turned to receive the same treatment. *Jesus* is the One who turned the other cheek and He was not weak. The question is: Was Jesus a fool, or was He revealing the laws of God for the Universe?

A mother went to the store to buy her child a toy. She found a puzzle and tried to work it herself. Then she turned to the clerk and said, "How can you sell this for a child's toy? I can't put it together." The clerk answered, "Oh, that's all right, lady. It is an educational toy to teach a child how to live in the world today. No matter how you put it together, it won't work."

By a Gallup poll several years ago it appeared that ninety-six per cent of Americans think they believe in God. Yes, they believe that God exists, but what good is it if they live as though He did not exist? Wouldn't we be more honest and somewhat less frustrated if we were godless?

Suppose we believed that all human history will be consummated in Christ (Ephesians 1:19) and acted consistently with that belief. If we accept God as the Creator of the universe we'd better take the rules that come with "the chemistry set." If we believe in God we will know by faith that "The things that are shaken are obviously things which can be shaken. They are thus revealed to be man made, passing, or temporal things by the very fact that they are shaken. And they are being removed out of the way so that the things which cannot be shaken may remain" (Hebrews 12:27), as quoted by Rufus Jones. (I asked him where he got it. He did not know.)

In this precarious day we must find the things which cannot be shaken.

Gandhi "gambled" his whole life on the belief that *love* and *truth* are the dependable laws of the universe. His followers took a vow for outgoing love, understanding, and against any form of retaliation or even bitterness. We lived in the midst of this movement for freedom in India and felt the mass power of it on the people. It was more than the power of one man over others. As one educated Indian woman said to me, "When we lived by this vow of love and truth we felt a power greater than ourselves take possession of us. It took all fear away from us and gave us a freedom which was not dependent on whatever happened to us." The West cartooned Gandhi in life, but in death they joined the whole world in awed mourning.

Who wins after all? And who is victim? Those who test God's law of love to the limit of their own margin of free choice find out. He is victor who is never circumstance-conditioned. He is victim whose reactions are determined by what others do to him. There is the twinkle of divine humor in Edwin Markham's lines:

> He drew a circle that shut me out,
> Heretic, rebel, a thing to flout,
> But love and I had the wit to win
> We drew a circle that took him in.

The business world says, "Courtesy pays." A man with difficult clients said, "I'll be courteous, even if it kills me." And it might, for if he doesn't have it in his heart, he will likely get it in his stomach — in the form of ulcers. Only genuine love and courtesy bring real results, all imitation attempts backfire.

Having genuine love is really a necessity of life. We often wonder why so many gates are closed to us. Perhaps the secret is here. Tagore, India's great poet, said, "He who wants to do good knocks at the gate; he who loves finds the gate open" (Collected Poems and Plays of Tagore, Macmillan and Co., Ltd., London).

The New Testament writings are always startling when we recall that they were all written out of experience. Listen! "Loved ones, do not put faith in every spirit, but put the spirits to the test whether they are from God; for many false prophets have been let out into the world. . . . You are from God, dear children, and have defeated them, because the One in you is greater than the one in the world. They are from the world, so they talk from a worldly point of view and the world listens to them.

"Beloved, let us love one another, because love springs from God and whoever is loving has been born of God and knows God. He who is not loving does not know God; for God is love. . . . Loved ones, if God loved us so much, we ought to love one another too. No one has ever seen God. In case we love one another, God remains in us and His love runs its full course in us. . . . We both know and put faith in the love which God cherishes in us. God is love, and he who continues in love continues in God and God continues in him. . . . Love has no fear in it; instead, perfect love expels fear, for fear involves torture; so he who fears has not reached love's perfection. We love because He first loved us. If someone says, 'I love God,' while he hates his brother, he is a liar; for he who does not love his brother whom he has seen, is not able to love God whom he has not seen" (I John 4).

A woman once said to me, "I wish you would pray for my sister-in-law to be more lovely so I can love her." I answered, "Sister, you have that turned around." The fact is we love others according to what we are and not because of what they are. God does not love us because of what we are, but because of what He is; and He is love. Jesus said, this was to be the distinguishing characteristic of His followers: "I give you a new command, That you love one another. By this everyone will recognize that you are My disciples, if you love one another" (John 13:34, 35).

Even though the love of God is a gift of the Holy Spirit, and the first fruit of the Spirit, still we must be apprentices in the practice of this love. Jesus even told us how to work out this love in our daily relationships. He knew it would take time for us to learn.

One of the most skillful apprentices in love was the man we called "Brother Rufus." Divine humor and unquestioned obedience to the way of love in his new life made him a real modern saint. He looked for the way of Jesus in everything, even when he was asked to conduct a funeral. He read all four gospels to find out how Jesus conducted funerals. To his surprise — "Jesus never conducted funerals; He conducted resurrections only!"

Another time he did find out exactly what to do. A misunderstanding developed between him and an old friend. He was greatly troubled because the friend refused to discuss the matter with him. He felt he had to do something, but he had no idea

what to do next. Then, to his delight, he found the next step
suggested in the eighteenth chapter of Matthew: "Take someone along and go again" (verse 16). Then he pondered, "Whom
shall I take? If I take a friend of mine he will think we are
ganging up on him, and then things would be worse than ever.
I know what I will do. I will take *his* best friend along, and I
won't tell my side of the story until we are all together." Brother
Rufus' choice of companion was the shock treatment which
opened the way to complete reconciliation. Brother Rufus said
to me, "What a Book! Imagine finding even the method of
procedure for love to work in reconciliation!"

"Matthew eighteen" has had a very definite place in the history of my own denomination. When I was baptized at eleven
I was asked to settle all differences with others "according to
Matthew eighteen" (meaning verses fifteen to seventeen): "If
your brother should act amiss toward you, go and show him
his fault privately; in case he listens, you have won your brother.
In case he does not listen, take one or two along, so that 'From
the testimony of two or three witnesses the whole dispute may
be settled.' If he refuses to listen to them, tell the church, and
if he will not listen to the church, treat him like a pagan and
a tax-gatherer."

I remember the impression given to me in many church
council meetings. When "the matter was brought to the church"
the story sounded like this: "He wronged me (tone of voice:
how terrible he is!), I showed him his fault (*good Christian
that I am*), but he would not listen. I took a witness along
but he would not listen even then (*he's a hard one!*). So now I
have brought the matter to the church according to the Scriptural method (*good brother that I am!*)." More often than not
the man did not listen to the church either, for by this time
he felt that everyone had ganged up on him. And the "righteous" ones became hard in judgment and the "sinner" hard in
self-defense. Something was wrong.

We don't talk about "Matthew eighteen" much any more.
We lost it because we missed its meaning as a method of love.
The only reason Jesus suggested going to the other brother was

to *win him*. This was made impossible when the going became self-defense and a blatant attempt to prove the other man wrong.

Also, in my youth, I got the impression that "let him be to thee as an heathen and a publican" was the end of the story, and the chapter was closed. In later years it dawned on me that a "sinner" is never dropped by Jesus. So this could never be the end of the story Jesus told. He would make another beginning. He said, "For the Son of Man came to seek and to save the lost" (Luke 19:10).

Jesus implies the same in the Matthew story: After saying, "Treat him as a pagan and a tax gatherer," He follows with: "I assure you, whatever you shall bind on earth shall be bound in heaven, and whatever you liberate on earth shall be free in heaven. Once more I assure you that if you are agreed on earth about anything for which you pray, it will be done for you by My heavenly Father. For where two or three have gathered in My name, I am there with them" (Matthew 18:18-20). If the real love of God is at work it might even be that the "two or three" that gather for prayer are the ones who attempted the reconciliation together. In any case, if the man is out of the fellowship, they are not to kick him, but to love him back through prayer and even heaven will honor this prayer of love.

If love motivates the procedure for reconciliation, forgiveness will precede the initial step as well as control the first attempt and any other attempts that might be necessary. Peter knew well that forgiveness was the crux of the matter. He said to Jesus, "Lord, how oft shall my brother act amiss toward me and I forgive him? Up to seven times?" What a saint Peter thought he was! The rabbis said that three times was enough to forgive anyone. Peter would give the man seven chances! But Jesus startled Peter by saying, "I do not say, up to seven times, but up to seventy times seven." To Peter this was, indeed, love to the uttermost. No leeway left for Peter to count to seven and then use his sword . . . or for me!

Before this whole conversation on reconciliation had taken place the disciples had come to Jesus asking, "Who really excels in the kingdom of heaven?" They still expected Jesus to

re-establish the throne of David and so they were greatly concerned about coming cabinet posts. This is why they vied with
one another for first place, even up to the shadow of the cross.

Jesus put a child in their midst and said, "Unless you become
converted and become as the little children, you will certainly
not enter the kingdom of heaven. Whoever, then, humbles
himself like this little child, he excels in the kingdom of heaven,
and whoever receives one such child in My name, receives
Me. But whoever is an occasion for stumbling to one of these
little ones that believe in Me, it were better for him to have
a millstone hung around his neck and to be sunk in the depth
of the sea."

This was strong language for Jesus to use, but, to Him, it
was tragedy to cause anyone to stumble. The one who "did the
wrong" may have been the "little one" and the one who caused
him to stumble was at greatest fault. He did not go in loving
concern because he was concerned only with his own prestige,
therefore he could not be helpful to the "weak one."

So far as the need for reconciliation is concerned the story
may be turned around. It may be that I am at fault, that my
brother feels I have wronged him. In this case, also, I must take
the initiative toward reconciliation. "So, when you are offering
your gift at the altar and remember that your brother holds
something against you, leave your gift there at the altar and
go, first come to an understanding with your brother; then come
and offer your gift" (Matthew 5:23, 24).

Suppose we followed this admonition literally some Sunday
morning. The minister would be standing on the church steps
with the offering plates beside him. The minister would say,
"If any of you are not at peace with any person, leave your
offering here (the church needs the money!), go at once, be
reconciled with your brother, then come back to worship."
There would likely be a small congregation that Sunday, but
it wouldn't be many weeks until the church would overflow.
Genuine love is authentic publicity and more contagious than
measles.

Spiritually practical James wrote to stumbling Christians who had difficulties in getting along with each other: "Where do conflicts and fightings among you originate? Do they not spring from your passions that are at war in your organs? You covet and you do not acquire; you murder and you quarrel and you cannot get hold; you fight and you battle and you do not possess, because you do not pray. You ask and you do not receive, because you ask wrongly; you want to spend it on your dissolute pleasures" (James 4:1-3).

There cannot be reconciliation and abiding love unless the real source of the trouble is discerned. Thus, this apprenticeship in love as we practice forgiving, both giving it and receiving it, becomes a training in honesty. It is astounding how hard it is, at times, to be honest, even though we have been taught all our lives to "tell the truth." I cannot be honest about "my brother" as long as I am concerned about my own prestige or my own interests. I cannot be honest about myself until I want to grow into maturity and into the likeness of Christ more than I mind the hurt of seeing my own imperfections. Seeing "my brother" without this undergirding love would lead to cruel judgment which would cause him to stumble and would make me hard. Seeing myself "as is" without remembering Christ's forgiving love would fill me with hopeless despair. But, thank God, this love is available.

Before Jesus came to earth it was rare for people to understand such love. The prophet Hosea lived in that day. He loved his wife, Gomer. She was unfaithful to him, still he loved her. She left him, still he loved her. Then one day he found her on the slave block in the public market place. He bought her back and reinstated her in his home as his wife and the mother of their children. His love would reconstruct her life through the mercy of his forgiveness. Then Hosea realized that if he could love Gomer this much, surely God's love must be so much greater and so much more redeeming.

We fare so much better than Hosea. Jesus Christ has come. We have seen His love, His forgiving love, His understanding love. His understanding makes forgiveness possible. Even on the Cross He prayed, "Father, forgive them, for they know not what they do." In the mirror of His love we can bear to be honest with ourselves and with others.

This practicing of love's honesty will reveal to us that love's forgiveness is not easy. We can no longer protect ourselves from hurt, for love is openly vulnerable to suffering. We must accept this suffering as Christ accepted the Cross. In fact, as long as we do not accept this vulnerability to suffering for another we have not forgiven fully. We are still bound by self, with its consuming self-pity. ("How could this happen to me?")

When a mother's son loses his way in life she does not even think of her vulnerability to suffering, she just suffers because she loves. If her husband loses the way it is much harder to forgive. For her to combine the redemptive love of God with the human feminine love reactions of a wife is, indeed, hardest of all. One beautiful woman I know is learning to do both. Concerning her otherwise very responsible husband she said, "I find myself in the depths when I concentrate on the inevitable irregularities. I am saved from it all when I stay close to Christ. My husband is so precious to me — I am not surprised that others are attracted to him. There are times when I would like to take him and his vanity and shake both good. But I feel better when I just love him." Redemptive love is winning.

Forgiving love is not an irresponsible love. Love forgiveness is not accepted or given casually or without sense of value. The Apostle Paul knew the value of this forgiving love of God and so he could not waste it. "It is through the love of God that I am what I am, and the love that He showed me has not been wasted" (I Corinthians 15:10, 20th Century Translation). When we know its value we cannot waste it, either. My part in accepting the grace of forgiveness from God is living in the grace of forgiveness in relation to all others.

Jesus taught us to pray, "Forgive us as we forgive." This is not a bargain with God, a trading of forgivenesses. God's love is the same in any case. His love can be limited only by my refusal to accept it. My refusal may not be in word, but in the condition of my heart. If my heart is tender toward others, it is open to Him, if it is hard toward others, the way is blocked for His entrance, too. All self-centeredness with its fruits of resentment and self-pity make me hard so that love is smothered out. So if I do not forgive others I have also made it impossible for me to *receive* forgiveness of God. But by His grace, as I forgive others I am able to appropriate His forgiveness. "Forgive us, Lord, as we forgive."

This forgiving love is not a superficial love. It does not "forgive" and carry resentment. Neither does it carry a form of forgiveness and at the same time push the sediment of ill will down into the roots of one's being. The forgiveness made possible by the gracious love of God is a gift and it makes its recipient genuine clear through, thus it is honest love.

A young mother with her beautiful babe in her arms told me of the resentment she carried for years against her family. This resentment kept her spiritually helpless for years. She prayed often in agony of soul for healing of her spirit, for she wanted to be a missionary with her husband. Then the miracle came. She described it this way: "One morning, as suddenly as the culminating birth of a child, and in much the same manner, a flood of forgiveness came to me. . . . The joy of new life was somewhat the same — tears of thankfulness came."

It is easier to forgive others than it is to forgive ourselves. While we are in the process of being honest with ourselves we often become overwhelmed by the gulf between what we are and what we ought to be. The farther along we are in spiritual growth, the more subtle the temptation grows to condemn ourselves. Our emotions may play tricks on us. We must not get lost in making comparisons with past experiences, but we must keep our eyes on the One who gave us forgiveness in the beginnning. He loved us while we were still sinners and we came accepting ourselves as we were, just as He accepted us. Now we must continue to do the same: "I am not yet perfect, I am in the process. I will not waste any energy kicking myself." It is pride that taunts me by saying, "After all this time, haven't you grown more than this?" But Christ says with loving encouragement, "You are growing. That is the reason you can see more things in your life that are not perfect. Let My grace continue to work, to cleanse and strengthen you."

"Everything that is exposed by the light is made visible and where everything is made visible there is light" (Ephesians 5: 13). The very fact that we can *see* our failures and shortcomings is evidence that we are in His Presence which is light. If the city hostess does not have time to dust the last minute before the dinner guests arrive, she would be wise to use candles. They shed less light and reveal less. The more light, the more that can be seen in our lives, too.

One day as I came down a Himalayan mountain path, I passed a dear little Christian woman who was so wise in the things of the Spirit. She said, "I want to tell you something: an *accusing* finger is never our Lord's finger." Then she went on up the mountain path. I do not remember her name, but I cannot forget her wise insight.

When pride accuses, the sense of guilt which follows is debilitating until it is recognized for what it is. When pride *accuses,* the guilt is general; when God *reveals,* it is specific. A trained conscience under the guidance of the Spirit is a moral and spiritual agency serving our growth. In the light of His love the recognition of failure is always accompanied with the forgiveness of His love.

This forgiving love is tender but not soft. It is honest but never merciless. It brings eternal hope, never retribution. It does not wink at evil or say, "It doesn't matter." It is the great "now," always a new beginning, unfettered by the past, set free to be God's child. Growth means constant renewal of life, which means we are always on the edge of new creation.

We can trust the Lord Jesus to give us this love when we remember that for Him it was costly grace, and for us it can never be cheap grace. We love because He first loved us. We love others because He loves them and us, too. We love because our acceptance of His Spirit makes this love the fruit of His life in us.

FOR FURTHER STUDY:

Read the First Epistle of John through.
Then read it again and list everything said about love.
Read I Corinthians 13:4-7, substituting your own name for *love*.
Rejoice that you can see where you are not perfect.
Practice using the love of God.

The book *Discovering Love* by Lance Webb (Abingdon) is very helpful.

CHAPTER 9

Joy, Peace

JOY AND PEACE are twin accompaniments of the love which is the fruit of the Spirit.

This joy is a different kind of joy from the joy of the child on Christmas morning. It is so much more than delight in things received. It is a joy that is outgoing with the deepest sense of worship. It gives one the sense of new life surging within, which it really is. The undergirding emotion of this joy is love because it is the fruit of the Spirit. Now for the first time one feels like loving the unlovely as well as the lovely. There is joy that the unlovely is no longer depressing. The joyous overflowing of love makes understanding and sharing spontaneous.

This spiritual exuberance of joy is especially evident when one comes into his first experience of union with God, through the Holy Spirit. Even though this experience may be packed with emotion, one's consciousness is not of the emotion, but of Christ. This may be called the "honeymoon period" in spiritual experience.

Then love begins its relentless and penetrating transforming of ordinary life, and the human mood becomes bewildered. The days bring so many inconvenient opportunities for love's demonstration, and one wonders if any love is left. The temptation of the new Christian, as of the new bride, is to say, "Joy is gone. Love is not the same. I am afraid it is gone." If joy is gone it is not because of difficult days, but because of the fear of its loss. Fear dissolved it. In the fear the whole attention was thrown onto the feeling in experience. Then when clutching at love and joy did not seem to restore the former feeling, fear increased.

Bewilderment would not have come if this new Christian had realized that emotions, or lack of them, are not the thermometer of spiritual status. The only thermometer of spiritual status is: "Am I still completely committed to do God's will?" Any reluctance to do His will can really bring the thermometer down. But emotional *feeling* is not the test.

A parable of what happens in such an experience came to me in a storm on the Mediterranean Sea. We were on a freighter which was completing a five-month around-the-world trip. Our ship had three motors, but only one was needed for full speed on a clear day. For a while we moved right along. In the midst of the Mediterranean we came into a terrible storm. The engineer used the power of all three engines, but with all that power we did not advance a knot for the records. It took three times as much energy to keep us standing still in the storm as it did to go full recordable speed on a clear day. But we were making progress because by standing still we were kept off the rocks of the North African shore.

As love matures, the joyous feeling of it will change, but it will be deeper joy as it becomes less superficial. The original exuberance stands out not only because of being new, but in contrast to the days before such joy was known. Love matures as it develops in the daily process of appropriation. Often much of love's energy, the Spirit of God, is absorbed in growing adjustments. Love is not gone, it has only gone deeper into the life. When this is understood, fear is gone, a new security develops. Even dark hours cannot obliterate love. With this understanding, joy also returns. But it is a joy of deeper quality. It has been tested and it did not get lost. Christian joy is never a fair-weather friend.

Christian joy is not an easy-going joy, either, as some seem to think. A handsome woman of great culture lost her husband and all of their wealth in Hitler's Germany. She and I were together one day when a mutual friend joined us. This mutual friend is a "bubbling over" Christian — "all is love in the world, just think love and all will be wonderful." When we were alone again, the woman who had lost everything said to me, "I wonder how much joy she would have left if she lost her family and her beautiful home!" That is the world's question, a suffering world's question. *If Christians never had losses and defeats the Christian witness would not be complete.*

Christian joy is no happy-go-lucky affair. It is more than the power of the mind over the body, too. I can remember when Coue came to America with his formula for a happy life: "Every day in every way I am getting better and better," to be repeated as oft as needed. A Washington city paper carried a cartoon while Coue was in town which said, "Day by day in every way I am getting better and better, but oh, the nights are awful!" Life's nights have to be taken care of, too. The joy of the day must have a carryover for the night, providing real rest, or the day's joy was mere pretense. This is the kind of joy that comes as the fruit of the Spirit. On the night before the crucifixion, knowing what the next day would bring, Jesus said to His disciples, "I have talked these matters over with you so that My joy may be in you and your joy may be made complete" (John 15:11).

On the same last night Jesus also said, *"Peace I bequeath to you; My peace I give to you. I do not give you gifts such as the world gives. Do not allow your hearts to be unsettled or intimidated"* (John 14:27).

The Apostle Paul was not in that group of disciples, but later through the Spirit he also found the truth of this great experience. While in prison he wrote to the Philippian church, "Be glad in the Lord always; again I say, be glad! Be known by all the people for your considerateness; the Lord is near. Entertain no worry, but under all circumstances let your petitions be made known before God by prayer and pleading along with thanksgiving. *So shall the peace of God, that surpasses all understanding, keep guard over your hearts and your thoughts in Christ Jesus"* (Philippians 4:4-6).

Through many years these words of Paul's had special meaning for me. When I left home for college and seminary to prepare for the mission field I had forty doHars and a faith that God would help me. However, I thought I should not bother Him with little things. Just before my first Christmas away from home I ran out of money. This was inconvenient, but *such an item would be of no concern to God*, I thought. Then one day I received a Christmas greeting from an old man in Virginia, whom I had met just before I left home. All he knew about me was that I was getting ready to be a missionary. On the inside of the greeting he had written, "The Lord put it into my mind and heart to send you this. Thank Him for it." And there was a money order for five dollars! Was God interested in such things?

My faith-boosting verses were these of Paul's. For years they gave me faith to talk to God about everything. And then it dawned on me one day that these verses say nothing about *prayer* being answered. (Of course other promises do.) But the promise is even greater: *We* are to be answered. "Tell God everything, have no anxiety, and the joy and peace of God will guard your heart in Christ Jesus." I felt almost as if God had played a joke on me in giving me these verses. But this is the divine humor of the kingdom.

Some people today try to get peace and joy through happiness pills. But the God who created man has a better prescription. The secret of His way is described in the list of "Blesseds" called Beatitudes which Jesus gave in the Sermon on the Mount (Matthew 5:3-10). These Beatitudes are a description of the characteristics of a true Christian. It is as if we walk around this man and see him from a different angle in different situations. Under each circumstance, sometimes rather astounding or ironic, the man is blessed. This is not a pill to give temporary happiness, it is real joy and peace given by God to make it possible to withstand anything that can happen. The "rewards" listed are not the motivation of this man of God but the inevitable issue of the character described.

"*Blessed* are they who sense spiritual poverty." Gone is the old nature of bitterness, resentment, retaliation, self-concern; come is the new nature of love. He belongs to the family of God.

"*Blessed* are they who mourn." But how could this be? I saw it recently in a very humble woman. She is so quiet and unassuming, one wonders how she can be such a strong leader in her church. Last year her church voted her "the woman of the year." The other evening I found the reason in her life. When her husband died, she felt like dying, too, she was in such despair. Then God came to her and gave her new life and comfort. She was so grateful she promised Him she would do anything He asked her, even if others could do it better. She was blessed and so is everyone who knows her.

"*Blessed* are the gentle" or the "meek." This is the craziest of all. Being "poor in spirit" toward God is easy to understand, but this is the same quality toward men. These shall "inherit the earth." We have seen too many counterfeits of meekness, all of them distasteful. The truly meek man is so fully given to God and His interest in men that no earthly power can manipulate him. He wins because he has within him that which cannot be conquered. The life of Jesus defines the strength of this quality.

"*Blessed* are the hungry and thirsty for righteousness." When children lose their appetites parents know they are sick. Hunger and thirst are a sign of health, but they must be satisfied or health is impaired. A great wave of spiritual hunger has gone over the world. Too many have never found satisfying food and drink and they have not been filled. Worse yet, when unsatisfied, they lose their healthy appetites. Has the church missed a great opportunity? Has she been too absorbed in her program, new buildings and her prestige, and too little concerned about sick humanity?

"*Blessed* are the merciful." Mercy is love in action. It is easy to be merciful when we are benefactors. The test of mercy as a quality of life is in our reaction to powerful people who know nothing but brute force or competitive undercutting. Can we be merciful to those whom we might otherwise fear? We will not know the power and joy of mercy and its mercy returns until we can have mercy, Godlike mercy for all.

"*Blessed* are the pure in heart." Purity means freedom from any admixture of base matter, as we speak of pure food and pure water. A pure heart is one that is singleminded in its desire to love and serve God. The opposite of the pure in heart is the "double-minded man, unsteady in all his ways" (James 1:8). The pure in heart shall see God. "You shall find Him when you seek Him with your whole heart."

"*Blessed* are the peacemakers." All the world wants peace, we just lack the peacemakers. Making peace is an art of love. Gandhi insisted that a climate of peace had to be created before anyone could make peace. Is that what is wrong with the world? We haven't worked on the climate enough? Peacemaking is not the same as "patching things up." Peace is a result of justice. We must make the justice and then there will be more climate for peace. We feel so helpless in regard to all the world trouble. But if the quality of peacemaker is ours it will begin in our own relationships. Only thus can we find the faith and hope for a greater peace. The real peacemaker truly belongs to the family of God.

"*Blessed* are those persecuted on account of righteousness." Now we have made the circle around this picture of Christian quality and we have the same result as in the first beatitude: ". . . for theirs is the kingdom of heaven." Some people have a persecution complex. They bemoan what people do to them. They are not blessed. Jesus is not talking about such self-centered bores. He is talking about those who lose themselves in the cause of righteousness and justice. These do not even know it when they are persecuted. The instigators of such persecution are usually those with vested interests and control in power blocs.

To the limit of his ability the peacemaker creates justice and makes no compromise with evil. The point of no compromise is the place of persecution. "Blessed are you when they slander

and persecute you, and *falsely* accuse you of every wrong because of Me. Be glad and supremely joyful because in heaven
your reward is rich; for they persecuted previous prophets the
same way."

The *joy* and *peace* which Jesus promised us the night before
He was killed are great enough to withstand anything that can
happen. "Delight thyself in the Lord."

FOR FURTHER STUDY:

> Read Paul's letter to the Philippians. It is a book full of joy
> and peace even though written in jail.
>
> The hymn book of praise for the early church was the Psalter.
> A few of the most inspiring ones are Psalm 46, 91, 103 and 146.
> Find the "blesseds" in them.

CHAPTER 10

An Even Temper,
Kindness, Gentleness

WE CAN THINK of this cluster of the fruit of the Spirit in terms of *patience* and *kindness*. A woman learning to drive said, "I can't learn with someone who has no patience with me." The patience of Jesus with Peter and the rest of the disciples is amazing. His patience with us is humbling. The very fiber of this patience is loving understanding and forgiveness.

Patience is the ability to wait, without irritation. It is much easier to push people — and circumstances. As we learn to wait on the Lord we can also wait for others. He lets us learn at our own speed. We must learn the same kindness for others.

Before the Apostle Paul knew Jesus Christ he was just as determined to do God's will as he was after Christ came to him. But before he knew Christ he was merciless toward all who did not see things as he did. In a great fever of zeal he attempted to get rid of all Christians in the name of God. When he knew the loving forgiveness of God his heart was melted and he saw the strength in this virtue of the Spirit.

Naturally easy-going people do not seem to need the grace of God to be patient and kind. But perhaps this is not the patience that Paul called the fruit of the Spirit. One brilliant professor was introduced at a banquet by a former student as a man of outstanding patience. The professor's wife sat with the M.C.'s wife and whispered, "I don't call it patience."

It takes special grace from God for an orderly person with a well organized program to have patience with those who slow down or thwart his program. The pastor who is a good program director will break before the one who takes life as it comes. He needs the gift of patience, and the other man likely needs the grace of discipline. The good shepherd pastor is the one who learns to put people before program and still have a program.

One young minister said, "There will never be progress in my church until our old moderator dies. He blocks all progress." The next day the old man had a stroke and almost died! He called the young minister to come to anoint him and pray for his healing. The young minister was in a panic. How could he pray after the way he had been feeling? He struggled all night in prayer. The next day he was ready to pray for the old man's recovery. The prayer was answered and the two became the best of friends and real co-workers. Love and patience made the difference.

Patience is sometimes called *tension capacity*. This makes one resilient without breaking. Without such resilience nerves get tense: "I can't stand it another minute." "If that telephone rings once more I'll go crazy." Tension capacity is an adult characteristic. Children cannot wait. They have to learn it.

Four-year-old Steven stayed with us while his mother was in the hospital. He was a happy boy until the fourth day. That evening he would not eat his supper and he would not let me come near him when he went to bed. He said, "I'll pray by myself." As I left him sobbing I thought, *Poor little fellow! He is missing his mother.* But later I discovered the ache was in his stomach and not in his heart. He had found a box of doughnuts and had eaten most of them! He was only four and this was a lesson on consequences. Perhaps next time he would be able to wait to eat properly.

Even so-called adults cannot stand to wait. They likely feel trapped by their own emotions. They cannot wait until others are ready and so they *force people to expedite programs.* They have no tension capacity, no resilience, no kindness.

Even mature adults fall into this hurry disease at times. The story is told of Phillips Brooks who was found one day pacing back and forth in his study. His friend asked his trouble. He answered, "I'm in a hurry, but God isn't."

A strong religious leader who does not have the love of God in his heart is liable to act like Paul when he was still called Saul. His teacher, Gamaliel, could wait to see if these Christians were of God or not (Acts 5:33-39), but Saul could not wait. "But Saul, still breathing out threat and murder against the Lord's disciples, called on the high priest and requested of him letters to the Damascus synagogues, so that, if he should find there any men or women who were of the Way, he might convey them shackled to Jerusalem." All this he was doing in the Name of God and to maintain the orthodoxy of the faith!

The love of God transformed this stormy strong man into a miracle of patience and kindness. He no longer pushed people, he could wait for them to find the way to truth. This didn't take less courage, it took more. Some vacillating leaders justify their wavering ways by Paul's "all things to all men." Paul never compromised to get a following as they do. His allegiance to God and the truth was greater than ever but the new love of God in his life gave him this winning patience and made him one of the great counselors of all time. His letters to the churches are letters from a counselor's heart.

To the Corinthians with their multitude of problems he described his counseling attitude: "Although I am free from everyone, I have enslaved myself to all of them *in order to win* a larger number. To the Jews I behave as a Jew *to win* Jews; to those under the Law as one under the Law, although I am not under the Law, *to gain those* under the Law. To those without Law I am as without Law — although not lawless toward God but committed to Christ's Law — *in order to win* those without Law. For the weak I have become weak *to win* the weak. I have become everything to everybody so that *by all* means I may save some. But I do it all *to advance the Gospel*" (I Corinthians 9:19-23).

"So, whether you eat or drink or whatever you do, *do it all to the glory of God*. So behave that you cause neither the Jews, nor the Greeks, nor the church of God to stumble, just as I myself please everyone in every way, *not seeking my own advantage, but that of the many, in order that they may be saved*" (I Corinthians 10:31-33). These words are out of an evangelist's understanding, counseling heart. This was no compromise of conviction, it was the sympathetic, patient understanding of love.

The tenderness of God in Paul is revealed also in his suffering for the Galatians when they became spiritually unorthodox. His yearning heart for them cried out, "My children, over whom I once more suffer birthpains until Christ is formed within you" (Galatians 4:19). Again, to the Corinthians after listing all the sufferings he had gone through for the Gospel, he added, "Besides these experiences from the outside, there is for my daily attention the care of all the churches. Who is weak without my being weak? Who is offended without my suffering grief?" (II Corinthians 11:28,29).

There is a legend about a woman who prayed to God for patience. In answer she received nothing but trouble. She then said to the Lord, "I did not pray for trouble, I prayed for patience." The Lord answered her, "How else will you learn patience, or even know you have it?" Growing in the love of God with its concomitant joy and peace is possible only as we let that love be tested by the hard things of life and so the love bears the fruit of even tempered patience, kindness and gentleness.

"Consider it wholly joyful, my brothers, when you get involved in all sorts of trials, well aware that the testing of your faith brings out steadfastness. But let steadfastness have full play, so that you may be completed and rounded out with no defects whatever" (James 1:2-4).

FOR FURTHER MEDITATION:

List your own needs in patience and kindness and then read
carefully:

Romans 5:3-6
II Corinthians 6:4-10
Colossians 1:11, 12
II Thessalonians 3:3-5
Hebrews 10:36
James 1:3, 4

CHAPTER 11

Goodness and Fidelity

ON FIRST THOUGHT it seems strange that Paul counts *goodness* as a part of the fruit of the Spirit in man when Jesus repudiated being called good even for Himself.

Then I remember that this statement of Jesus was made in answer to a question from the rich young ruler. Jesus always answered inquirers beyond their articulated questions. He was a nice young man. He was evidently willing to share his wealth, he was exemplary in every way from man's standpoint, but from God's standpoint, he withheld himself. The neighbors said he was a "good young man" and he likely felt the same way about himself. But he did not know about the goodness that comes from God alone. Jesus saw his real need and asked, "Why do you call me good? No one is good except one, even God." Then Jesus asked the "good young man" to give up all his possessions, and then to come follow Him. "At this suggestion he felt stung and went away saddened" (Mark 10:17-22).

When Paul said *goodness* was a fruit of the Spirit he was not inconsistent with the inference of Jesus to the rich young ruler. Paul remembered only too well that the more one knows of goodness the greater the conflict in his own life grows until he finds the goodness which God alone can give.

"The Law is holy and so is the command holy, just, and good. Did then what was good in itself become death to me? Not at all. Instead, it was sin that must be shown up as sin, by working fatally for me through something good, so that through the command sin might become immeasurably sinful.

For we know that the Law is spiritual; but I am fleshly, sold under sin's control; for I do not understand what I am working out. I practice not what I want to do but what I hate to do. Now if I do what I do not want to do, I agree that the Law is good. . . . I know that within me . . . what is good is not at home; the personal willingness is there, but not the accomplishing of what is commendable. For I fail to do the good I want to do and I practice the bad I do not want to practice. . . . For in my inmost heart I admire God's Law; but in my whole natural makeup I notice another law, battling against the principles which my reason dictates. . . . Who will rescue me from this body doomed to death? Thanks be to God because of Jesus Christ our Lord. . . . There is now no condemnation to those who are in Christ Jesus. . . . If then the Spirit of Him who raised Jesus from the dead, dwells in you, then the Resurrector of Christ Jesus from the dead will through the Spirit that dwells in you make also your mortal bodies live. It follows then, brothers, that we are obligated, but not to our earthly nature to live under its control, . . . for as many as are guided by God's Spirit, they are sons of God" (Romans 7:12-8:14).

Some people recognize the *"presence"* of Christ in their lives when they become, through His grace, members of the family of God, but they limit the power of His Spirit to presence only. They do not acknowledge the possibility of any intrinsic change in the nature of the new Christian. Such a doctrine seems like an alibi for not growing more Christlike. The Scripture teaches otherwise. "For His divine power has bestowed on us *every requisite for life and godliness*. . . . so that *you might become sharers of the divine nature*, having escaped from the corruption in the world that arises from passion" (II Peter 1:3, 4). And Paul also said, "We all are *changed into the same likeness from one degree of glory* to another, derived as it is from the Lord's Spirit" (II Corinthians 3:18). "If any one is in Christ, he is a new creation. The old is gone. Look! The new has come" (II Corinthians 5:17). "Having stripped off the old

nature with its practices, and having put on the new self that
is being renewed to have knowledge in the likeness of Him
who created it . . ." (Colossians 3:9, 10). And the purpose of
the indwelling Christ in the heart (Ephesians 3:13-19) is "so
you may be filled up to the whole fulness of God."

Whatever goodness is possible in man is possible only as the
Spirit has freedom to work out through the life. As the old
nature is changed into the new nature, goodness is also the
fruit of the Spirit. A Christian psychiatrist says the real work
of the Holy Spirit is in the unconscious. Paul would agree,
I am sure: "That He may grant you . . . to be empowered with
strength in the *inner self* by His Spirit . . . that you may be *rooted*
and *grounded* in love . . . so you may be filled up to the whole
fulness of God." Goodness is intrinsic in the Spirit. Say "Yes"
to the Spirit and goodness follows.

The real work of the Spirit in one's life is as quiet as the
growth of a flower. It will usually be an unconscious process,
too. Our responsibility is continuous, deliberate response to
Christ. The result of the Spirit's work may be as much a surprise to us as it is to those who know us — the joy of discovering that the practices and reactions of the old life are no longer
natural.

I just received a letter from a lovely mother of four lively
boys. God gave her His Spirit. . . . "At last I saw my real problem: All my twenty years in Christ I had lived on my love for
Him, but now I claimed God's love to be my very own and
I would never again have to work at loving from myself. . . .
This is such a simple and wonderful thing to live so long without. This morning it became clear what had happened to me.
Day after day, as I washed my breakfast dishes I saw my neighbor leave for work. Before, I always thought, 'There goes a
man who doesn't love God.' Now for the first time my thought
was, 'There goes a man whom God loves dearly.'" Only those
with like experience know what a revolution in disposition this
brings. It takes one off the judgment seat and puts him on
the mercy seat.

The only thing that can hinder the growth of this new life within is to choke it by returning self to the center. Such a return can happen unwittingly. For the paradox of this life in Christ is that one is more conscious of his shortcomings than of his "holiness" or goodness. This is because as the Spirit of God permeates the personality more things are revealed that are not good so that they can be exposed to the work of the Spirit also. If we permit anxiety to enter into this process we return self to the center. But if we continue to look to Him His love works for more goodness in us. This process is called *sanctification*. It means we are *set apart* for God.

Fidelity or faithfulness is the *staying power* after the first rapture is over. This fruit of the Spirit is not dramatic. It is "pressing on" no matter how dark the road. Dark periods in life are training times for faith. We need have no anxiety about dark days. They will not stop Christian growth, they will strengthen it. However, anxiety will stop growth. It is the opposite of faith. It is diseased imagination while faith is healthy imagination. "All sunshine makes a desert" is the wisdom of an old Arab proverb.

"Naked faith" is faith indeed. Nothing is left but the faithfulness of God, but that is everything. "For I am convinced that neither death nor life, neither angels nor mighty ones, neither present nor future affairs, neither powers of the heights nor of the depths, neither anything else created shall be able to separate us from the love of God that is in Christ Jesus our Lord" (Romans 8:38, 39).

After all, the Spirit of God isn't given to us merely to make us feel good. The Spirit is power for service. The evidence of the presence and activity of the Spirit will come with every opportunity for service. Sometimes when God has a special task for us which would be fruitless without His power, He may let darkness come to us so we don't forget to look to Him. More than once in the presence of a congregation I have felt that I, too, was part of the congregation receiving a blessing from God.

I wasn't the channel through which He came to the congregation. He came direct to each one. This is as it should be. Without question the power is God's.

A misinterpretation of darkness may cause much heartache. A ministerial student who had been saved from alcoholism came to school with a vibrant witness to God's power. He was not prepared for any change in his joyous exultation, unless he would feel more of it. One day in class he blurted out, "I have lost everything I had when I came here. I don't feel like I did at all. How can I ever be a minister? I have no witness left."

About that time I heard of an alcoholic who was trying to find new life. Those carrying a concern for him said he needed experience in a Christian family. So I asked this student if he would invite the poor man to his home for dinner. He did so the following Saturday night. In the next class period I asked about the Saturday night guest. The student told a wonderful story of fellowship, understanding, and of sharing what he knew about the power of God to save a man from sin. He told of his little son's joy in the guest who knew all about circuses. As he told of his assured faith that God would redeem this man, I said to him, "I see that there is nothing wrong with your joy in the Lord this morning." He looked bewildered a moment, then he said, "Oh, I forgot all about my own feelings!" The man who came to dinner has been truly redeemed and the student is now a happy pastor.

Faithfulness in the life of faith is never irresponsible. "God will take care of it" does not mean the same as "Let George do it."

One man lived by faith, he said. Actually he was lazy and improvident. When he got into a corner he sponged on anyone with a half open door. He never considered anyone else's convenience. To let him get away with it was not true brotherliness, but how to help him or circumvent him was a real problem. He was very clever at making others appear heartless if they did not jump night or day to meet his needs. Sharing with him was a one way transaction, his way only. This is not faith or faithfulness.

This man's action was not related to the God-given faith of men like St. Francis of Assisi or George Mueller of London. Mahatma Gandhi lived in poverty like an Old Testament prophet. His poverty was dynamic fidelity to a cause. He figured out how much each person in India would have if everything were divided evenly. He would never go beyond his share for the day, even when an American guest gave him special fruit. He truly loved all people and they loved him. Mrs. Naidu said one time, "Yes, Gandhiji lives in poverty, but no one knows how much it costs the rest of us to keep him in poverty." She and others loved this mutual responsibility with him for they shared like concern for the same cause.

Sorrows may be conquered, frustrations may be met creatively, but the crucial test of fidelity is *defeat*. Unfortunately, "success" is a requirement in our western culture. Even ministers are classified as successful or unsuccessful. How many modern pulpits would accept the Apostle Paul, or even Jesus Himself, as pastor?

If there had been headlines in Jerusalem Good Friday evening, they might have read: NAZARENE DEFEATED AT LAST BY RELIGIOUS LEADERS. It did look like defeat at the time. But we know better now. That was not defeat on Good Friday. It was the greatest victory ever won on earth. We are the disciples of that Victor and shareholders in His victory if we remain faithful.

FOR FURTHER CONSIDERATION:

> We can ask ourselves some questions whenever we feel "below par":
> > Is there a physical reason?
> > Is there a personal relationship failure that needs restoration?
> > Is there any slack in faithfulness to Christ?
> > Have I moved back into my own orbit in any measure at all?

Then:

Reaffirm the fact of God's faithfulness and infinite love.
Reaffirm my personal commitment to Him.
If it is still dark, rest in the Lord.
Even if it is dark, He is there.
Perhaps I need an emotional rest.
Joy cometh in the morning!

CHAPTER 12

Self-Control

NEARLY EVERY DAY we read about someone who committed a crime and excused himself by saying, "I couldn't help it." Whether he was emotionally drunk or liquor drunk makes little difference, so far as the consequences are concerned.

The subject of liberty is a very important one in the world today. But the story is too often as in the early days: "While they promise them liberty, they are themselves slaves of corruption; for a *person is a slave to whatever overpowers him*" (II Peter 2:19).

The Stoics found it a nuisance to be under the power of any passion. They said reason should be in control at all times. But too much stifling of emotion made for a cold existence or despair at failure to live up to what reason dictated.

It is said that it is a disease of our culture that people have not learned to make their own decisions and so they are a prey to whoever would manipulate them. Actually, those who have not learned to choose for themselves either succumb or rebel. In neither case are they free.

There is only one way to be free and that is to accept God-control. It seems like a paradox, but it is true that only under God-control can we have self-control, only then is the human will free to make choices. God always honors that freedom of choice. This is the reason *self-control* is the fruit of the Spirit. "For God has not given us a spirit of cowardice, but of power and love and self-control" (II Timothy 1:7).

St. Francis de Sales' favorite prayer was, "Yes, Father! Yes! and always Yes!" This is flying "on the beam." I shall not forget the first time I flew through clouds. I was thankful the pilot had a beam to go by. We need not fear when God is at our controls.

All these characteristics which are a fruit of the Spirit are emotions — emotions of the real self, the "new creature." The first of these emotions was *love* and the last of the list is self-control. Self-control is the balancing of them all and the sum of all. Another word for this would be *poise*. Next to love, poise was the outstanding characteristic of Jesus' emotional life. All His emotions were intense but always in perfect equilibrium without strain. He was never upset by anything. Through the Spirit we may grow in the same way.

In the first days of commitment to Christ it is easier to be ascetic than to refrain from it. One wants to give all. Then as the realization grows that many things are returned to us (Matthew 6:33) it is easy to go to the other extreme and pay too much attention to the "added on" things. The poise of self-control is always keeping Christ and His way first no matter what is added. Paul found out that asceticism without love was worth nothing whatever (I Corinthians 13:3).

Prosperity throws more people off balance spiritually than poverty. This is the reason real stewardship is so essential for every Christian. A "tithe" helps a lot, but it is not stewardship. Stewardship involves all we are and all we have. What we spend on ourselves, if we belong to God, is given to Him also. The real question is not having or doing without, it is, does it all belong to God?

The minister whose services go to the highest bidder has his values mixed up, but the other fellow who must take the lowest bidder is also mixed up. One young minister had the choice of three churches. He had a wife who was just getting adjusted to giving up the beautiful home and excellent job her husband left when he was "called" to the ministry. They had four children, too. One of the churches that called him had a poor parsonage, poor school facilities, poor salary, the "best" one had a very good parsonage, near a good school and an adequate salary. He came to me greatly troubled. Wouldn't he be selfish to take the "best" church? He felt impelled, because he wanted to give all to Christ, to take the poor church. I assured him that poverty was no argument *for* anything anymore than adequacy was an argument *against* something, besides God was more concerned about his family than he was. That left him free to choose. God sent him to the place that was best for his family and used him greatly through many years in that city.

Throughout church history there has been a swinging back and forth between "beauty" and "austerity" in dress and architecture. Pride has just as free rein in austerity as it does in beauty. Simplicity is the balanced virtue. In simplicity there is no room for ostentation or ugliness; in fact, simplicity is beauty.

Self-control, or temperance, is more than mere policing of the wrong desires and hungers. Before Paul listed the fruit of the Spirit he described the opposite way of life which shows the drastic need for the Spirit and its fruit. "You have been called to enjoy liberty, brothers; only, do not let the liberty be an incentive for the flesh; instead serve one another by way of love" (Galatians 5:13). The liberty in Christ had taken the Galatians out of the "fear control" of paganism. They weren't mature enough yet to control the new freedom, so it became license. "License" is self-centered: "I can do as I please." The way back to center is "serve one another by way of love."

Then (verse 16 ff.) "It comes to this: behave in a spiritual way; then you will not carry out your fleshly cravings. For the longings of the flesh are contrary to the Spirit, and those of the Spirit are contrary to the flesh; they are in opposition to each other, so *that you will not do just what you like*. But *if you are guided by the Spirit* then you are not under the Law."

The real issue is, then, not between the right and wrong desires; the issue is between Christ and self. If self belongs to Christ and the Spirit is in control, then there is *control of self*

by the Spirit. This is real Christian self-control. The new
desire brought in by the Spirit bears the longed-for fruit.

"If we live by the Spirit, let us also be directed by the Spirit"
(Galatians 5:25).

FOR FURTHER THOUGHT:

Read II Peter, chapters 1 and 2 for the description of the
new disposition and its development.

Read James 2 for a possible surprise.

Read James 3 for the most unruly member and consider its
control.

Avoid all anxiety. It closes the door to the working of the Spirit.

God has patience. Let Him have a chance.

Part III

LIFE THREATENED

They conduct all their activities to be noticed by men. They broaden their embroidered prayers and enlarge their law-reminding tassels; they cherish the chief place at dinners and the front seats in the synagogues, the greetings in the markets and to be called "Rabbi" by men.

— Matthew 23:5-7

CHAPTER 13

Danger of Spiritual Cancer

MY BROTHER HAS JUST BEEN TOLD that he has cancer. We all feel, "It can't be." Here are cells that ought to be good but they are out of control. If they cannot be controlled they break the whole equilibrium of the body, even to death. To date man has not found the cure.

The greatest danger to spiritual growth is much the same. It isn't the "sins" that are generally recognized as sin that pervert the "good" man from his center in Christ. It is an overemphasis on some part of religion to the extent that the heart of true religion is destroyed. It is "retaining a form of piety" but remaining "strangers to its power." Or "having a form of godliness, but denying the power thereof" (II Timothy 3:5, K.J.).

Holding the form of religion without realizing the original meaning has been the story of all religious history. A Brahman friend in Bombay told me this story:

In ancient India there was a devout Swami who lived in the forest with his disciples. This Swami was especially proficient in his meditative powers. He spent hours every day lost in his meditations about God. One day a little mouse scampered around the room and distracted him greatly. He could not risk having his devotions spoiled again, neither would he kill the mouse. But what could he do? Finally, he decided to bring a cat into the room. To keep the cat from killing the mouse he tied the cat to a post. This worked fine. The cat was quiet, the mouse stayed away, and with his back turned he could forget them both. So every day the Swami tied a cat to the post before he began his meditations.

Years went by and the Swami died. His disciples had loved him very much. They wanted to do everything just as he had done it. Then they began to wonder about that cat. They had never asked him about it, but the cat must have had something to do with his great meditative powers. So they decided that one of the tenets of their religion would be to tie a cat to the post whenever they went to meditate.

Again years passed. Now the religious councils of this group were taken up with discussions on: "what kind of a cat to tie to the post"; "what color it should be"; "how long its tail should be"; "how far from the post it should be tied"!

The man who told me this story had never read church history!

A Christian minister told me about the time his church had a serious debate on singing hymns as well as Psalms in church. One night in church council an old brother with a long white beard (and tobacco juice running down its length) got up and said, "I will never sing hymns in church. I will sing Psalms only. When I go to meet my Lord I want to meet Him with *clean* lips!"

The religious leaders who brought Jesus to trial were very strict in all the observances of their religion. In order to avoid ceremonial defilement before the great Passover Feast they would not enter the Roman court, but they could railroad an innocent man to death. They wanted Him out of the way for His ministry threatened their prestige. Besides, He wasn't orthodox by their reckoning.

Shortly before this Jesus had warned His disciples and the crowds about such leadership: "Do and observe whatever they tell you, but do not behave as they do; for they talk and do not practice. . . . They conduct all their activities to be noticed by men. For they broaden their embroidered prayers and enlarge their law-reminding tassels; they cherish the chief place at dinners and the front seats in the synagogues, the greetings in the markets and to be called 'Rabbi' by men. . . . But your greatest shall be your minister; for whoever elevates himself shall be humbled, and whoever humbles himself shall be elevated . . ."

Then directly to the proud leaders: "Alas for you . . . hypocrites, for you traverse sea and land to make one proselyte and, when he becomes one, you make him a son of perdition twice worse than yourselves. Alas for you, blind leaders . . . because you tithe mint, dill, and cummin, and omit the weightier aspects of the Law — justice, mercy, and fidelity. . . . You resemble whitewashed tombs; they appear beautiful on the outside, but inside they are full of dead men's bones and every impurity. So you seem to men outwardly upright, but inside you are full of hypocrisy and lawlessness" (Matthew 23:1-39).

Usually these discerning words are read from the pulpit in a vindictive voice. But Jesus did not say them like that. He spoke out of a broken heart; "Jerusalem! Jerusalem! murdering the prophets and stoning those sent to you! How often have I wanted to gather your children as a hen gathers her chicks under her wings; but you were unwilling." This is the heartbreak that led to the Cross.

Another time Jesus told a story for such leaders: "And he spake this parable unto certain which *trusted in themselves that they were righteous, and despised others:* Two men went up into the temple to pray; the one a Pharisee, the other a publican [one an honored spiritual leader and the other a socially despised man]. The Pharisee stood up and *prayed thus with himself, God, I thank thee, that I am not as other men are,* extortioners, unjust, adulterers, or even as this publican. I fast twice in the week, I give tithes of all I possess. And the publican, standing afar off, would not lift up so much as his eyes unto heaven, but smote upon his breast, saying, God be merciful to me a sinner."

Then Jesus added that the social outcast went away justified rather than the great religious man (Luke 18:9-14, K. J.).

Long ago I heard about a nun who said, "After living with

saints for forty years I can understand why Jesus spent so much of His time with sinners." And then there were the two monks going down the corridor, each crowned with a halo. One monk said to the other, "But I am holier than thou!"

These stories make us chuckle, but it is always easier to see the truth in others. When we think we are holy we may be farthest from holiness in God's sight, for when we think we are so good, we actually are self-centered and not God-centered.

One morning the newspaper joke for the day was: "There are two kinds of people in the world: the good and the bad — and the good decide which is which." I laughed heartily until it dawned on me that this was more than funny. It was really an indictment, an indictment against *self*-conscious religion.

Self-conscious "goodness" makes a mockery of true religion. These are the ones who are *confident of their own* "goodness." The other side of that coin is: "looking down on others" or despising others. "I am good, they are bad." The more I think about this, the more I realize that my impatience with people "who ought to know better" is too much related to this "despising others." I'm glad I finally found this out.

The tragedy of too many in the church is in this self-conscious "goodness." These are the ones so taken up with their own spiritual selves and deeds that they have no room in their lives for the love of others. They never "sacrifice" except for spiritual prestige. This is what Paul was talking about when he said, "Though I give all my belongings for nourishment (to the needy) and surrender my body to be burned, but I have no love, I am not in the least benefited" (I Corinthians 13:3).

When I was a child it seemed that one of the pet themes for the preachers was the judgment scene in Matthew 25:31-46. They emphasized the *judgment* part of the story. Since then I have heard it used almost entirely as a plea for *service* to the needy. Now I wonder! The good people in the story did not know they were good. They kept asking, "When did we do all this?" They had met the needs of others because their hearts were full of love. They had not kept a diary of their

good deeds to keep tab on accrued merit in heaven. The re-
jected ones did not expect rejection. They must have thought
they were good, Perhaps, after all, the basic point of Jesus'
parable is the *unself-consciousness* of service done in love even
more than the division between "good" and "bad" or the service
rendered in love.

Is it possible that even our church expansion programs might
sometimes be more an impersonal glorification of our own group
than true evangelism flowing out of a heart that loves God, to
people who need God?

Several years ago two men sitting back of me on a bus were
discussing a headline in the evening paper. A certain church
conference had just set a goal of five thousand new members
the following year. One of the men said vehemently, "I'll see
to it that I am not one of their statistics!"

A young girl felt the impersonal fever of the seasonal fervor
during the town "revival." Church members who never talked
to her the rest of the year came begging her to come to church.
Her hungry soul cried, "They don't love *me*, they just want
to add me to their numbers." This is not the way Jesus loved
and won people.

The "self-conscious virtues" are the ones that *drive* us. They
put us under compulsion to be religious: "I must be good"; "I
want to be a saint"; "a great power in prayer"; "a great worker
in the church"; "I want people to see Jesus in my face." Or,
"I must win for I am the man of God in this group"; "I must
be unselfish" and worst of all, "I cannot admit that I am wrong
after the spiritual witness I have given."

The "self-conscious virtues" are also the ones that wear us
out. *Trying* to be good is the most devastating job on earth.
This is what led to Paul's cry of despair, "O wretched man that
I am! Who shall deliver me from the body of this death?" He
found the deliverer.

We say it another way when we are caught at acting below
the image we hold of our "good selves." "Now, how did I ever
say anything like that? I am not that kind of a person." (Our

families might answer, "That's what you think!") Or we might say, "I don't know what got into me, I never did such a thing before." And so around the vicious circle we go, adding despair to futility — unless we, too, find the deliverer.

This "professional" Christian needs a vacation from his profession just as much as any other professional person. If he doesn't have one he'll explode at times at home, or get sick. Whenever we strive in our own strength to close the gap between what we have to admit we are and what we know we ought to be we become entangled in the vicious system of pride. This pride is merciless. We become hard toward others who have the same weaknesses we are reluctant to face in ourselves. We fall into despair if we are caught in failure without a religious alibi. We fall into dishonesty if no alibi is available. All decisions and reactions are made according to self reference.

The picture of this religious person with his "self-conscious virtues" is not attractive. No one who starts sincerely in his religious life wants to get off on this road. But perchance, if anyone is headed toward this road, he may read the warning signs along the way. Recognize the signs and the way back will be clear:

Feelings easily hurt.
Sense of humiliation at any failure
Loss of interest when not appreciated
Anger when thwarted
Cleverness at showing one's self to advantage
Impatience with others
Irritation when opinion is not accepted
Defensiveness for one's own position
Compulsion to fight those who do not think as I do
Despising others
Blaming others
"I am holier than thou" attitude ("Can't help it, I
 am better!")
Self-pity
Chronic discontent
Inertia, sense of powerlessness

In all this array self is still, or again, the center. The greater the pretense, the greater the sense of futility. There are others who have only a mild case of this trouble, but it is still crippling. A sweet missionary friend in India was so concerned about her own spiritual development that she could not get her mind off herself. For years this anxiety continued. She feverishly attended every spiritual retreat possible. She did all the things suggested for spiritual development. She still had anxiety.

One day I told her about my cousin and his peanut patch. He was only eight years old and he did not know it takes peanuts a long time to come up. Every day he visited his garden and still no sign of peanut plants. He decided to investigate. "Lo! the peanuts were growing toward China!" So he went over the whole plot and turned every plant over so that its roots stuck out in Virginia!

The last time this missionary friend was on furlough I had a wonderful day with her. She was radiant with her enthusiasm for new India, for the church there as the Indian Christians were taking more responsibility. After several inspiring hours with her I could not resist saying, "Ruth, do you realize that you have not said one word today about your own spiritual development." She laughed with joy. All the old anxiety was gone because her whole attention now was on Christ and His work, and not on herself.

Another subtle danger to mature spiritual growth is the all too easy transfer from consciousness of Christ to an emphasis on the *doctrine* of a relationship with Him. Love slips away with this transfer. We may be more orthodox than ever, theologically, but we will no longer be spiritually orthodox. One of the evidences of this regression is that we find ourselves *fighting* for the truth instead of *witnessing* to it. We become hard toward those who disagree with us instead of reaching toward them with a loving yearning. We find ourselves judging the deeds of others with no effort whatever at understanding what led to the deeds.

Jesus cut through every social taboo of His day to reach

people who wanted a better life. It was the orthodox religious people that made life hard for Jesus and it was they who put Him to death. We do not want to be in their company.

We had an Indian friend who was a professor in a large city college. He had been one of Gandhi's closest disciples in the early days. His close relationship to Christianity began with his friendship with C. F. Andrews, a missionary saint whom all India loved. Later he joined the wider Quaker Fellowship. He followed in the Spirit of the Lord Jesus, but many would have hesitated to call him a Christian.

One evening Mr. Sinha came to our home for dinner. We had eggplant curry which he enjoyed very much. I told him this was what we had for our meal at our communion service in India. He was surprised and said, "A meal?" I said, "Yes, we have a meal, and feet-washing, too." Then I added, "We are going to have one next Sunday night at our church, would you like to come to watch?" He answered, "Not watch, I'd like to take part." I told him to come, but did not tell him of my fear that someone might try to keep him away from the Lord's table. I would not tell him unless I had to. How would one explain about "closed communion" to someone who reads the New Testament on its face value and does not know church history?

I called our pastor the next day, told him the story and asked if this man who loved Jesus could come to the service. He answered, "Jesus never pushes any seeking man away from Him and this is His table."

Mr. Sinha took part in the whole service. Later that evening, in our home, he sat in great reverence. He said he was never more deeply moved. "And a white man washed my feet," he said over and over again. Several weeks later he phoned to ask, "When will you have one of those services again? It did something for me that is good for me."

A few days after this Mr. Sinha had a stroke in the midst of one of his class sessions, and he died three hours later. We are so thankful that that last touch he had with the Christian church was in harmony with the love of Christ.

In many Moslem homes in India every door has a mirror on it, but each mirror is covered with a curtain. I asked a Moslem neighbor why they covered their mirrors in this way. She said, "If we pray in that room and happen to look in the mirror and see ourselves we cannot think about God."

Perhaps this would be a good parable for Christians. Do we "behold as in a mirror the glory of the Lord," or ourselves?

FOR FURTHER STUDY:

Read the Sermon on the Mount (Matthew 5-7) and list the things Jesus said that will make religion genuine and keep one from becoming a hypocrite.

For psychological help in understanding the New Testament teaching about self, to date, I have found most helpful and discerning: *Neurosis and Human Growth*, by Karen Horney (W. W. Norton & Co.).

CHAPTER 14

Diagnosis and Cure

IF ANYONE FEELS DISCOURAGED about his own spiritual growth or that of the church, let him take courage from Paul's correspondence with the Corinthian church. Paul knew how far the Corinthians had to come to attain maturity in Christian character. He knew the kind of religious experience they had had before they became Christians. Before, they had constant fear of evil spirits, great emphasis on methods of contriving emotional ecstasy and frenzy in religious worship, idolatry with its concomitant immorality in Corinthian temples, and a completely different ethic for daily life.

Paul also knew of the new experience they had had in Christ since they became Christians: "Daily do I thank my God for you for the divine grace that has through Christ Jesus been granted to you; for in Him you have in every respect been enriched, with full power of expression and with adequate knowledge. God is reliable, through whom you were invited into the companionship of our Lord Jesus Christ, His Son" (I Corinthians 1:4-9).

But now Paul has had reports about the church, that the old life was catching up with them, but in the forms of the new faith. They were quarreling among themselves, they were even competitive and arrogant about their gifts from God! Their new freedom in Christ became license to such an extent that they were worse than pagans on one moral issue. Love in Christ was perverted to leniency with evil in their midst. Hero worship of Christian leaders became a substitute for the Lordship of Christ and then they quarreled about their heroes. Others went to the other extreme and repudiated the "pleasures of this world" and advocated asceticism as an end in itself.

Paul knew this was a Christian community which still had in it genuine zeal and enthusiasm despite all the faults and failures. They had come to the place where they needed clearer discernment on the relation of Christian experience to its individual and group emotional accompaniments. Paul wanted them to know the difference between Christian *experience* which could become an end in itself and *experience of Christ* which would always keep Christ central.

Paul's faith in the work of the Spirit was so great that he could write to these stumbling Christians: "To the church of God at Corinth, those made holy in Christ Jesus and *called to be saints*" (I Corinthians 1:2). He wrote to them with the loving patience of a counselor's heart, hoping to give them the ethical values they needed without spoiling any of their spontaneity of expression. He wrote to restore their sense of values in the gifts they so coveted. He attempted to safeguard their unity in Christ while he set them free for all individual variety possible.

Out of all the correspondence with this church the most familiar part is the thirteenth chapter of I Corinthians, the "Love Chapter." We respond to its cadences more readily than we do its message. Perhaps that is because we forget it was written to a church stymied in its growth by conflict and emotional excesses. This chapter is the heart of Paul's appeal to bring them back to their spiritual senses. It was seriously written for daily living, and it is just as applicable to us today as it was to that struggling church so many years ago.

Even though I speak in every human and angelic language and have no love, I am as noisy brass or a loud-sounding cymbal. Some were so appealing in their oratory that they naturally commanded a following. Others had quite a reputation for ecstatic speaking. Paul didn't tell them to be less oratorical or less ecstatic; he told them that no experience, even if it rated a following, was worth anything without love. The test of its authenticity was in whether the desire was for self-display or for Christ's honor. Those who spoke in the Spirit would verify in their witness that *"Christ is Lord."* This meant that the gifts of the Spirit were not for mere emotional satisfaction, nor for display, but *for the common good.* It meant that although not all had this gift, still *each gift was of value.* There should be *variety,* but there should also be *unity* in the Spirit and in the same Lord. Each had a responsibility to every other one. If Christ was Lord, then love would rule.

A handsome minister was introduced as the greatest orator of his city. He had such great appeal that his church was filled every Sunday night, as well as in the morning. He was counted as a very successful minister. I heard this same minister describe the beauty of his church. In eloquent words he described the altar and then added, "When I am before that altar the place is empty. I am a clanging cymbal. My heart is empty. I need the love of God in my life. Pray for me." This prayer was answered.

And although I have prophetic gift and see through every secret and through all that may be known . . . and have no love, I am useless. Corinth was in a country where intellectual prowess was greatly honored. There was a great interest in occult mysteries. Even though some in their church had gifts of understanding and prophetic insight, in Christ they could claim no special prestige. Without love even these gifts were worthless.

If I have sufficient faith for the removal of mountains, but I have no love, I am useless. We know today that even mere subjective faith has real value. The attitude of faith is healing in itself. I heard a man say one time, "I have great faith. When I pray for someone to get well, he gets well." Then someone asked, "Is everyone you pray for healed?" He answered, "No, but then it is because *they* lack faith, mine was not at fault." I wondered what this accusation would do to the sick person. This man seemed more concerned about the prestige of his faith than for those for whom he prayed. Nevertheless, even when faith works, it is of no spiritual value without love. With love it is the power of God.

And though I give all my belongings for nourishment to the needy, but I have no love, I am not benefited. I have heard it said that the way to get people to give for charity and even for the church is to publish what they give. God knows how the hungry and destitute of the earth need help, no matter how it is given. Perhaps we have to cash in on the pride of people if they are not mature enough to care about the needy! But the fact still remains that this is of no spiritual value to the donor. Had Paul heard what Jesus said? "When you do benevolence, do not blow a trumpet ahead of you as the hypocrites do in the synagogues and in the streets to gain glory from men" (Matthew 6:2).

Publicized giving, which would not come otherwise, is good money to use, but it is not stewardship. If we see what Paul saw we will enjoy what "Brother Rufus" said on stewardship, "Feed a cow good and it will be a relief to her to be milked."

And though I surrender my body to be burned, but I have no love, I am not in the least benefited. This is asceticism as an end in itself. Desperate people who know no other way but the merit system to find God are pushed to asceticism. The more they suffer, the more merit they expect to receive. But it is hard to understand how anyone who had experienced the grace of God would fall into this kind of suffering. There is just as much possibility of being proud of poverty as there is of being proud of riches, only the pride in poverty is likely to be for religious reasons, and therefore it is worse. Whenever the reason is self-centered pride and not love, there is no spiritual value in the attitude or action. Whenever the emphasis is on the giving rather than the one to whom it is given, love is not the motive. Jesus was poor, but He was never an ascetic.

This description of love was strong language for the Corinthians. Perhaps today we would understand it better thus: One can be theologically orthodox, believe all the right doctrines, be the most dependable member of the church, be the biggest giver in the church, be one of the most esteemed leaders in the church; but if self is still the ruling factor in life, if prestige and honor are determining factors in all actions and reactions, then love is absent and all this service is of no spiritual value.

Take Paul's test in the love quality:

Love endures long	I endure long
Love is kind	I am kind
Love is not jealous	I am not jealous
Love is not out for display	I am not out for display
Love is not conceited	I am not conceited
Love is not unmannerly	I am not unmannerly
Love is not self-seeking	I am not self-seeking
Love is not irritable	I am not irritable
Love does not take account of suffered wrong	I do not take account of suffered wrong
Love takes no pleasure in injustice	I take no pleasure in injustice
Love sides happily with truth	I side happily with the truth
Love covers up everything	I cover up everything
Love has unquenchable faith	I have unquenchable faith
Love hopes under all circumstances	I hope under all circumstances
Love endures without limit	I endure without limit

"Love never fades out." Even though I have grown away from childish ways there is so much more to learn. When I am finally face to face with Him I shall understand fully. "There remain, then, faith, hope, love, these three, but the greatest of these is love." Make love your great quest, then aim for spiritual graces.

After all, Paul was not discouraged with the stumbling Corinthian Christians. His final appeal was a reiteration of his first evangelistic message to them when they first accepted Christ: "First and foremost, then, I transmitted to you what I have received, that Christ died for our sins; that also He was buried and that He arose on the third day" (I Corinthians 15:3, 4).

This is ever the tremendous appeal of the love of Christ for us, He died for us. Even death could not conquer Him. He arose from the dead. He is a Living Lord. Not only did He appear a number of times to the disciples and others, but after the Ascension He appeared to Paul himself, as to one untimely born.

This is the glad news for us today: Jesus is alive and contemporary. Paul introduced people to Jesus Christ, to His living presence and to His available power. He presented no argument about a dead person, but an encounter with a Living Lord.

FOR FURTHER STUDY:

Read the Corinthian Letters. List the problems in their church and the answer of Paul to each problem. Paul was not discouraged, we need not be — since we have a Living Lord.

Part IV

LIFE NURTURED

I am the Living Bread that came down from heaven. If anyone eats of this bread, he will live forever.

Just as the life-giving Father sent Me and I live through the Father, so he who nourishes on Me shall live through Me.

— John 6:51, 57

CHAPTER 15

Food for Life

FOOD FOR THE PHYSICAL BODY is an important item in daily living. Just as important is food for the spiritual body. Loss of appetite is a cause for real concern in either case. Even many who consider the Bible as spiritual food do not know how to use it as food.

One day in India I was called to visit a sick woman. Although her name was on the church roll she never showed any interest in the church, nor did she bother to read the Bible. But she was quite ill and she turned to the Bible. However, she thought all that was necessary was to hold it in her hand. When she would fall asleep it would fall out of her hand. When she awoke she would be frantic until she could get it in her hand again. For her the Bible was magic only. She paid no attention to the Living Word, she merely used the book as a charm.

The old Moslem woman who lived across the road from us was nearer the truth. She was considered a saint by all the Indians who knew her. In fact, she looked saintly. Even though she was over eighty years of age, she still spent five hours daily in silent worship and in the reading of her Koran. (Five hours of silence daily would contribute some saintliness to any woman!) Maji (meaning honored mother), as everyone called her, became a very good friend of mine.

One day when I was sitting on the floor with her our visit was interrupted by a poor village woman whose child was ill. She asked Maji to heal her child. Maji wrote a verse from the Koran in ink on a small piece of paper, then she put the paper in a bottle of water and gave it to the woman. She said to her, "Tomorrow give this water to your child to drink, and God's words which will have come off the paper into the water will heal your child."

This made me think of Ezekiel. The Old Testament prophets were living parables. Ezekiel's story is very dramatic: "As for you, son of man, hear what I say to you; be not rebellious like that rebellious house. Open your mouth, and eat what I give you. When I looked, there was a hand stretched out to me; and see, a written scroll was in it! He unrolled it before me, and it had writing both inside and out. He said to me, Son of man, eat this scroll; then go and speak to the house of Israel. So I opened my mouth and He had me eat the scroll. He said to me, Son of man, eat this scroll which I am now giving you; fill your stomach with it and digest it! Then I ate it, and it was in my mouth sweet as honey" (Ezekiel 2:8-3:3).

Our concern is how to get spiritual nourishment out of the Bible so that it will be the Living Word for us. Jesus gave the basic answer to this concern when He said, "I am the Bread of Life. Your ancestors ate the manna in the desert and they died; this is the Bread that comes down from heaven, so that anyone who eats of it may not die. I am the Living Bread that came down from heaven. If anyone eats of this bread, he will live forever. And the bread which I will give for the life of the world is My flesh.

"Then the Jews wrangled with each other: 'How can this person give us his flesh to eat?' So Jesus told them, Truly, I assure you, unless you eat the flesh of the Son of Man and drink His blood, you have no inner life. He who eats My flesh and drinks My blood has eternal life and I shall raise him up on the last day; for *My flesh is genuine food* and *My blood is genuine drink.* He who eats My flesh and drinks My blood remains in Me and I in him. Just as the life-giving Father sent Me and I live through the Father, so *he who nourishes* on Me shall live through Me" (John 6:48-57).

We do not wrangle, we know this is not cannibalism. But

we do ask sincerely how to eat spiritual food. This means more than holding a Bible in one's hand or buying enough copies to make it the world's best seller. It means more than reading it through several times a year to beat someone else's record. When we read it properly something will happen to us. In fact, a great friend of ours said, "If the Bible doesn't shock you, you haven't read it." This is what the writer to the Hebrews meant: "The word of God is living, effective, and sharper than any two-edged sword. It penetrates even to the dividing line of soul and spirit, of joints and marrow, and is skilled in judging the heart's ponderings and meditations" (Hebrews 4: 12, 13).

We can join the Psalmist in his plea: "Teach me, O Lord, the way of Thy statutes and I shall keep them to the end. Give me understanding, and I shall observe Thy Law, and keep it wholeheartedly" (Psalm 119:33, 34).

Even more clearly did the Apostle Paul see this as he understood the work of the Spirit of Christ: "And He has qualified us to be ministers of a New Covenant, not of written law, but of a spiritual nature; for the letter kills, but the Spirit makes alive" (II Corinthians 3:6). We may follow the law of God in exact imitation, but if it is not done in the Spirit of Christ it will have no effect on our lives. Anyone who is literate can read the words of the Book, but only the same Spirit by which the words were inspired can give meaning to those words. The "letter kills" when the words are imitated without entering into the spirit of their meaning.

The proper understanding of God's Word comes, then, through the work of the Holy Spirit. "Through the Spirit, however, God has revealed it to us; for the Spirit examines everything, even the deep things of God. For among men who knows a person's thoughts, except the man's own inner spirit? Similarly, no one knows the thoughts of God, except the Spirit of God. And we have received, not the spirit of the world, but the Spirit that comes from God in order that we may realize the graces that have come to us from God. . . . The worldly-minded person does not accept things of the divine Spirit; to him they are folly and he cannot understand them, because they are estimated from a spiritual standpoint" (I Corinthians 2:10-16).

To have spiritual understanding does not mean that this faith approach excludes the intellect. God gave us minds to be used. He never does for us what we can do for ourselves. He will never give us a special vision to tell us what we can find already revealed and written in His Word. Some people have, foolishly or out of laziness, misinterpreted Luke 12:12, "For the Holy Spirit will teach you at the very moment what you ought to say." They seem to think that they should not study ahead of time what they will speak for God. They do not note that this promise is from Jesus for the hour when His witnesses are arraigned before the authorities for being His disciples. One mountain minister said he had to come to the pulpit empty so God could give him the message. Sometimes he missed the point of the Scripture as much as he did the hole in the baseboard which he aimed at with his tobacco juice!

It takes spiritual skill to be thoroughly prepared and still be open to God for new ideas or even changes in thought. But the mountain minister is not the only one with this problem. A brilliant seminary student said to me, "When I try to be spiritual my grades slump, when I try to be academic I get snappish and secular. In my efforts at reconciling the two I get pessimistic and neither spiritual nor academic."

When we come to God with our whole being we bring our minds to His Word and our hearts to Him. He and His Word are one, so we never need to vacillate from one approach to the other but we can do both at once. It is also highly important for us to know the content of God's Word as already revealed. God has a much better chance at guiding us in today's problems if we already are familiar with what He has told other people. More Bibles are sold today than ever before, but it often seems as if Christians know less about its contents than ever before.

So many Christians today are bewildered by "every wind of doctrine." Even the devil quoted Scripture, so we know it can be misused. We want to be led into all truth. We don't "know it all" yet. We need not be afraid of new ideas or new truths. We do not want to miss anything, neither do we want to lose any good thing we have. As we learn all we can, we should constantly appraise what we know in the light of His Spirit. We throw no present idea away until we have something better in its place. The disciples made many mistakes because they did not understand about the Kingdom Jesus preached. But Jesus waited for them to have the light of the Holy Spirit after Pentecost. When they saw the real truth they sloughed off their old theological ideas so easily they hardly knew when their ideas changed.

What we need to discard may not necessarily be wrong, it may be merely inadequate. We want all God has for us and so we let the new truth take care of the old, and thus we grow in knowledge as well as in faith.

When we feel bewildered about any truth or teaching we can learn from the saints who talked about "centering down." We hunt for the central underlying fact that we can be sure of and then stand on that and look around at all the other ideas which have bewildered us. But now we can look from where we are standing, which is on what we *know*. The blind man in the ninth chapter of John is a good illustration of this. He had reason to be bewildered. He was healed of his blindness and then enmeshed in a theological battle. Even his parents didn't have the courage to stand by him. When cornered by the religious authorities he was still unruffled. He refused to get caught in the theological conflict, then answered, "One thing I do know, that I was blind and now I see" (v. 25). This was the one thing that could not be argued and he took his stand on that fact. When Jesus heard what was happening to him, He found him and the man was ready to accept Him.

Many people use the Bible only a verse at a time. Bible verses are wonderful, especially when they are the "promises."

They may even happen to be right when chosen by chance. When I was in college I heard a lecture by the woman who signed herself "The Country Contributor" in the *Ladies' Home Journal*. She told of an unhappy Saturday in her life. The neighboring women had gone on a picnic when she still had all her cleaning and baking to do. The children were constantly underfoot that day. By evening she was in a welter of self-pity. She threw herself down on the couch in despair. Then she remembered three chickens she had penned up under a tub in the yard. She thought, "They can just smother and my family can do without chicken this Sunday. I won't do a bit more work today!" Then suddenly she remembered what a friend told her to do in trouble, "Open your Bible at random, run your finger down the page to the seventh verse and do whatever it says." As she thought of this her curiosity began to work. So she tried it. She said to us, "Believe it or not, my finger landed on 'Rise, Peter, kill and eat.'" This coincidence struck her "funny bone," courage came back with her laugh, and she got up and killed and dressed the chickens and lost her self-pity.

This stunt is all right for a game, but it is not a dependable method for guidance on any issue. Also verses alone may have little meaning without consideration of their context. Or they may even mean much more taken in context. I suppose no verse has meant more to a busy mother than "In quietness and confidence shall be your strength" (Isaiah 30:15, 16). No matter what the circumstance, quietness before God and confidence in Him are appropriate and will bring strength to any one. This is always relevant for any individual. But if we will look at the context of this verse we will have to do a turnabout in our thinking about the real principles that govern our world and our national security. The admonition to quietness and confidence was not to an individual but to the nation in great danger from a stronger power. They made an alliance with another great power and depended on this alliance rather than on God and the moral and spiritual strength He would give.

The prophet said they were trusting in "oppression and crooked-
ness" (v. 12) rather than in God. The question, then, that
we must face is: Do God's laws of love, truth, integrity apply
to individual relationships and break down when it comes to
national relationships? This verse then has a spiritual bomb-
shell in it. "In conversion and rest you shall be saved (from
Communism?); in quietness and confidence shall be your
strength."

If we accept the prophet's thesis we begin our Bible consideration with a great faith: God did create this world. God
created man. Therefore all truth in the universe is God's truth
and the laws for man's being and his development were made
by the Creator of man. The Bible is the story of God's relationship with man and it gives us the rules and directions and principles the Creator made for His creation. These laws are in the
Bible because they are true, which is a much stronger statement
even than to say, "They are true, because they are in the Bible."
God is greater than His Word, for He is first.

The Bible is the personal history of God's redemptive relationship to man and of man's intermittent response to God.
From the very beginning God took the initiative in establishing
a relationship with man. In fact He limited His own power
by giving man the right of choice to obey or disobey. God did
not want puppet worship from man, He wanted chosen worship. God waits for man to find his way and for him to choose
the right way. God has done much waiting, for the refrain of
the Old Testament story seems to be, "My people are a rebellious people!" In Isaiah 30 it was, "But you would not." God
wants to do us good, but He can do it only as we let Him.

In order to understand the story of God and man we need
to understand some of the history of His Holy Book. First of
all, the Bible is not really one book, but a library of sixty-six
books written over a thousand-year period. God used all kinds
of people to do His writing. No man's individuality was blotted
out by the Spirit of God, so even in the story of Jesus we have
the Gospel *according to Matthew*, the Gospel *according to Mark*,

the Gospel *according to Luke,* the Gospel *according to John.*
(And today men read what is written in our lives *according to
us.*)

Although written originally in Hebrew, Greek, and Aramaic
the Bible has been translated into over eleven hundred lan-
guages and dialects. The story of these translations reads like
a mystery drama full of plots laid by prejudiced minds while
men of God worked to bring the Bible into the language of
every people on earth. Just as God protected His original communication, so He continues to protect His Word through all
translations.

Young people are often greatly disturbed about the Bible
and the science they study in school. Since God created this
world it is all His and so there cannot be conflict between one
part of His creation and another part. Bewilderment comes
when we forget that the Bible is concerned with *why* there
is a universe and science with *how* the universe works. The
Bible is the supreme record of God's redemptive activity. Faith
in God means that we will not be upset by anything, and we
will not be afraid to seek His truth everywhere.

Even though the Bible is a library of books most people see
it as a whole and feel bewildered by its size. They don't understand the strange customs of other peoples in ancient lands. It
is important to know about all the peoples of Bible times. We
can well wonder how Abraham came into a belief in one God
when all those around him believed in many gods and wor-
shiped idols. Legend says that even Abraham's father was an
idol maker. His faith really means something to us when we
realize what he was up against in all his surroundings.

We accept Abraham as a symbol of a man of faith, but when
we read his story, we are surprised at some of the things he did.
We wonder how a man of God could act that way. Why did
he tell a lie and above all, why did he listen to Sarah when
she asked him to father a child by her maid? That would be
scandal today, but in Abraham's day it was not unusual. In
fact it was accepted, for a man had to have a son, one way or

another. To us it is the strangest of all that the wife made the suggestion. This is one time when a man should not have listened to his wife. God had made him a promise. (And what a chain of events came from that lack of faith. The big troubles in the Middle East today are between the descendants of Sarah and of Hagar, the maid!) However the surprise is still not that Abraham lived according to the culture of his day, but that *he lived so far above the culture of his day* in his faith in one God. The miracle is that God could reach through to him at all and that he was willing to leave his country and go out not knowing where he was going.

Then consider King David. On the way to church one Sunday a friend asked me about King David. She had the whole story of David to teach in her Sunday school class that day. Finally, I asked, "Do you mean to tell me that you are teaching about David and you haven't read all the Scripture about him this week?" She answered, "Oh, I know about him, I saw the movie, *David and Bathsheba,* this week." I said, "But you can't go by that. That was censored." David's affair with Bathsheba wasn't news in his day. That is the way kings did things then. The news item in the story is that David had a conscience on the matter. The culture of his day did not give him that conscience. All kings of that day took pride in their war prowess as well, but David had a conscience about this, too. He could not build the house of God because his hands were bloody. The miracle is that David could hear the Voice of God in matters at variance with the culture of his day. Of course David had the Ten Commandments and the Law, but as a king he might have said "God's laws don't work in the political field" as so many people do today. But David humbled himself before God and man because of his sin. Hollywood gets many "Bible stories" from Bible characters wherein they were a normal part of their culture but the part of the Old Testament which is a background for the New Testament is the part where these people lived *above* the culture of their day. This we know from the way Jesus used their Scripture.

The greatest part of the Old Testament is the account of the prophets and their messages from God. They discerned and spoke the eternal truths of God as relevant to contemporary and transient situations. They believed all of life had to be lived by the principles of God. Even when the nation had deteriorated spiritually, morally, politically, and it looked as if there was no hope, the prophets came with an assurance of national hope—but only in turning back to God and His way of life.

With the prophets there was always a remnant of the faithful but the people at large continued to be a rebellious people. They did not understand what God was like, and they seemed helpless in their ignorance and sin. So God did more for man. He sent His Son to live on earth. Jesus came and lived God's principles of life here on our very earth among people very much like us in their longings and struggles.

We miss the strength, the courage, the keen discernments, the daring, the unprejudiced love of Jesus when we do not know about the people that surrounded Him. When we know what His teaching meant to those people to whom He gave it, it means much more to us today and helps us greatly in making it relevant to our problems.

To know more about Jesus we read the Good News in Matthew, Mark, Luke and John. When we come to the nineteenth chapter of John we marvel as we remember the fifty-third chapter of Isaiah. How similar they are! As we have seen, after a short sojourn on earth as a man, Jesus left the earth so that the Holy Spirit of God could come in a way never possible before. This coming (Acts 2) was an event in history. When we want to know what this coming of God in the Spirit means to ordinary people we turn to the book of Acts and all the rest of the New Testament, which is mostly letters to new churches made up of growing Christians.

The Apostle Paul did not know Jesus on earth, but met Him as we do. He was the first one to take the Good News of Jesus to a people of another culture. In going to the Gentiles he had to decide what was Jewish culture and what was distinctly Christian. He is known as the man with the "mind of Christ" and his basic message was that Christ can dwell in the human heart: "Christ in me." The great problem in the early church was whether the Gentiles had to become Jews before they could become Christians (see Acts 15). When we understand what discernments he made between the culture of his day and the heart of Christianity we can learn how to make the same discernments today.

The story is reversed when a missionary from the West goes to an Eastern land. Over a hundred years ago some felt that new converts should change clothes and other customs to be more like the western church, when they actually were more like the people of Jesus' day on earth than we are in the West. And the question arose in India as in Corinth about the observance of holidays. The Hindu New Year is a festival of lights. When the early missionaries asked the new Christians not to observe this festival the Christian homes only were in darkness, everywhere else there was light. Somehow this was wrong. Only Christians in darkness? So Christians also had lights everywhere as everyone else did, and this became the supreme time of the year to go into the bazaar and preach about Jesus the real light of the world. This is the way Paul had to think through the problems of his day. By the same Spirit guidance we can find our way.

So before we can get the greatest spiritual help from the Bible we need to know it well. There is no time to waste if it is now a closed book. Start. And keep on. But start where? You might begin with the book of Mark. It is short. Read it for Jesus. How did people feel about Him? What did He do for and to them? What happened to Him? Read the whole story in one sitting just as you would an article in a magazine. Then read Luke the same way. Luke was a doctor. He had great interest and sympathy for people. He saw the warmth and love in the ministry of Jesus. Luke wrote two books. Read Acts for his continued story of Jesus, present now through the

Holy Spirit. See how Peter now differs from the man who failed His Lord even after all the training he had with Jesus. See what happened to a very religious Pharisee when he became a Christian. Watch to see "what made Paul run." And so we might take each book of this wonderful library God has given us. It is about real people in everyday human relationships. It is most of all about God and the coming of His own Son to earth to live and die for us so that we can be new creatures. It is a Book to be taken seriously in every part of our lives.

Read it, whether you feel like it or not. It will do something for you. Then someday when the Spirit of God comes into your inner being a new desire for God's Word will be born in you and a new understanding will be given you. A little girl was asked what she had learned in school that day. She said, "I learned a lot of things I did not understand and then I learned to understand them."

We must eat the Word so that we may be nourished in our given relationship with our Living Lord and so that we may grow in that relationship.

FOR STUDY:

Follow suggestions already given in this chapter.

CHAPTER 16

Guidance for Life

THE BIBLE is not only the story of God reaching out to redeem man, but the story of how He has communicated with man. What has already been revealed needs no duplicate revelation from God. This is the reason we should know the Bible well.

The way of love, truth, purity, and integrity are already revealed. Self-centeredness, pride, arrogance, impurity, evil desire, anger, slander are already condemned. When confronted with any of these there is no hesitation one way or the other as to which to follow.

There are frequently stories in the paper of people who blame God for their spurious "guidance," like the man who was baptizing his thirteen-year-old daughter in the river. He said God told him to hold her under the water so she could go to heaven in this hour of holy purity and avoid all the temptations of this world. He ignored truth already revealed.

There are times, however, when one way looks as good as another; the issues are not clear, many facts are not known, and yet a decision must be made. The perennial questions are: "Can I get guidance from God as the men of old did? Does God still communicate with man? If so, how does He do it? How do we hear it? Can we be sure concerning any course of action, especially when one way looks as good as another?"

A group of young people wrote out their questions about guidance. Here are some of their concerns:

"How can I distinguish between selfish desire and the urging of the Spirit?"

"When intelligence and emotion are in conflict, how can I find a basis for integrity?" (especially when choosing for marriage?)

"How can I discern intuitive guidance when it seems in conflict with the practical?"

"Can I depend on the work of the Holy Spirit in my unconscious when I may still be limited by unconscious difficulties?"

"How can I know if an inner compulsion is a pressure of circumstances, an unthought-out following of childhood patterns, or the real pull of God?"

"Can I have overdependence on God and underdependence on personal effort and responsibility?"

"When do I accept a circumstantial 'no' as final and when do I go on to overcome a difficulty?"

"How do I choose between seemingly good things?"

In the Old Testament prayer is most frequently recorded as a conversation: "And God said to Moses and Moses said to God," but there is more of God's side of the conversation than of man's. The prophet's main message was always, "Thus saith the Lord." It is often told that little Samuel said, "Speak, Lord, for Thy servant heareth." But today we say, "Listen, Lord, for Thy servant speaketh."

In Corinth the women were the ones who talked too much, but in our day everyone talks too much. When everyone talks, no one is listening.

A man came to visit us one day. He talked so much we could do nothing but listen. He was very interesting and we enjoyed him, but we were greatly amused when he bade us good-by and said, "Thank you so much, you are great conversationalists!" Many people determine their opinion of God by their own talking. When they are out of talk, they think they have lost everything. Laryngitis could knock their religion out the window.

The people who are in despair when they have no audience have a hard time learning to worship. For them the most excruciating punishment is solitary confinement. My mother used to say, "They have no mental furniture." Some scientists say we must discover inner space now. Life isn't all a TV channel where silence is not permitted. A listening ability is one of the greatest needs of today.

The first discipline for guidance is this listening ability. For it, one must first practice silence. Silence may be passive, but it need not be. Listening is a very positive, active quietness. And when God enters man's silence, that silence becomes pregnant with life.

As listeners we face the question, "Is the God who revealed Himself to the men of Scripture known to us only by report? We have that great holy record, but does communication from God to man stop there?"

If God no longer communicates to man, then God has changed, or man has become impossible to reach. But even from Scripture we know better.

Jesus said to His disciples, "I have still many things to tell you; but you cannot take them on now. When He comes, however, the *Spirit of Truth will guide you* into every truth" (John 16:12, 13). Later, on the Day of Pentecost, after the Spirit had come, Peter said to the people: "The promise is to you and to your children and to all those far away, as many as the Lord our God may call" (Acts 2:39). We are the people "far away" so we have the assurance of this guidance also.

There is a communion with God in which we are silent before Him and have all our relative values adjusted according to God's evaluation. Without this quiet communion we get our price tags all mixed up.

When we practice this communion with God it becomes possible for God to have communication with us as He did with the early Christians. Listening for God's communication to us is an adventure of faith, indeed. We have the same living Lord, the same Holy Spirit, the same God of the universe, and we are the same kind of people.

The New Testament story will whet our appetites for this

assured guidance through the Holy Spirit. It will also help us
to understand the possibilities of communication from God to
man.

The most astounding guidance after the coming of the Spirit
was that which seemed so natural to the disciples and yet was
so different from their regular experience only a few months
before.

There was the lame beggar at the Beautiful Gate in Jerusalem (Acts 3). He was there every day and the disciples must
have passed him daily, for they continued to worship in the
Temple as they had done before. But this day when the poor
man begged for money, Peter and John looked at him and
said, "Look at us." The man did, expecting a coin, but Peter
said, "Neither silver nor gold is mine, but I will give you what
I have: In the name of Jesus the Nazarene, walk!" There was
no hesitancy on Peter's part, this seemed as natural as handing
out a coin. No wonder the man forgot Peter and John and
thought only about God!

When persecution came, Peter and John did not have "guidance sessions" to know how to avoid difficulties. They said to
the authorities, "Whether it is right in the sight of God to listen
to you rather than to God is for you to judge; as for us, we
cannot refrain from telling what we have seen and heard" (Acts
4:19, 20). In this experience the communication from God
seemed to be intuitive. It was their new natural reaction to
a situation of need and a situation of danger which followed.

When deacon Philip became an evangelist and was in the
midst of a successful meeting in Samaria, it took more than
intuition to take him away from such a success to send him out
on a desert road where one would not expect to meet any man.
"But an angel of the Lord told Philip, 'Rise up and about
midday go down the road that runs from Jerusalem to Gaza — a
lonely road.'" The remarkable thing here is not the means of
communication, the "Angel," but that communication could
be made, and that Philip was sensitized to respond to this guidance rather than to stay with evident success. This move would

look foolish from a secular standpoint. Leave a meeting like that and go down to a desert road! But Philip went. The only articulate information he had was to go.

When he got there he found an important man from Ethiopia on his way home from worshiping in Jerusalem. He was sitting in his chariot reading the prophet Isaiah. "Then the Spirit said to Philip, 'Go up and contact that chariot.'" Now the communication is by way of "the Spirit," likely through Philip's inner hearing. Now Philip the evangelist counselor takes the initiative and asks, "Do you clearly understand what you are reading?" The man did not, and he invited Philip to sit in the chariot with him and teach him. And one more hungry soul went from the searching of the Old Testament to the Good News of the New Testament. A spiritually needy man on a lonely road and God could get a busy man out of the busy city to come to meet his need! If we were better listeners, would more of today's spiritually hungry people have the help they need?

The next communication story is about Saul. He was the last person who might be expected to hear the voice of Jesus. He was determined to destroy this new "perversion of Judaism." Only God knew that Saul wanted most sincerely to do God's will. He just had his theology crooked. The religious man who is stubborn in his interpretation is often God's greatest problem. It took extra light to change Saul. He had to hear an articulate voice to know that the Jesus he persecuted was the Living Lord. The evidence of his integrity is in his complete change in his interpretation concerning Jesus Christ without any consideration of his own prestige. A vision or a cataclysmic experience does not mean that a man is more greatly honored by God than one who never has any such experience. It just means that this man was harder to reach, but he was honest and God wanted him and because of his integrity, could break through to him.

Ananias was one of the disciples in Damascus. He knew why Saul was coming to Damascus. So it took a "vision" to reach through to Ananias to send him to meet Saul's new need. God would not do for Saul what another Christian could do for him. It must have been evidence doubled to Saul when, in his blindness, he heard a man enter his room and lay hands upon him and say, "Brother Saul, the Lord sent me, Jesus who appeared to you on the road you traveled, so that you may recover sight and be filled with the Holy Spirit." And the most violent enemy of the new Faith became its most ardent evangelist. Again God did only what man could not do and from there on reached men who could do the rest of the ministry.

The next story of making connection between the spiritually needy and someone to help is the story of Cornelius. Cornelius was a military officer of the Italian "occupying army." Even though he was a Roman he believed in the God of Israel (Acts 10). So God communicated to him with an articulate message as to the man who could help him. He was given Peter's name and address and told to send for him. The miracle is that he heard and sent for Peter.

It took another special communication to get Peter ready for these Gentiles. The new Christians had not yet learned how little their new faith was dependent upon their old traditions. They did not yet know what to discard of the old as they went forth in their new faith. They did not yet know what of their manner of living was of prejudice and what was of conviction. Learning this was just about as hard as it was for Saul to turn to Jesus as the Christ.

While the men were on the way to get Peter they were likely wondering if this Jew would accept them since they were Gentiles, and if he would come with them. Peter was on the housetop praying. His food was being prepared downstairs and he was hungry (at least he did not grouch but used every moment for prayer while he waited!). He fell into a trance and, of course he dreamed about food. But what horrible food! Everything a Jew was forbidden to eat!

I never knew how Peter felt until I sat in front of a boy on the train in Manila who was eating a duck egg. (To prepare: keep in warm straw nine days, then cook. .To eat: break the end with the juice, drink it from the shell; then break the shell and eat the embryo!! Scientifically, perfect food. Want some?) That's how Peter felt, but the communication said to him, "Rise, Peter, kill and eat." Three times the voice spoke and said, "What God has purified do not you consider unclean." By this time Peter thought this must have some special meaning.

While Peter was still trying to figure out whether this all meant something, *the Spirit said to him,* "There are three men looking for you! Rise, go below and travel with them unhesitatingly, for I have sent them." So Peter went down and said to the men, making it easy for them, "I am the one you are looking for. On what account are you here?"

From there on the connection was made, Peter went with them and had a wonderful experience in the home of Cornelius. The presence of the Spirit there was recognized even by the Jerusalem church as Peter reported back to them. And the first opening was made to separate Christianity from the Jewish culture of that day. It took visions to get this accomplished. The miracle was not in the visions, but that God could break through to these men to help them into new ways of thinking and new ways of living. Growing in a sensitivity to the Spirit is as much of a miracle, it seems, as original birth into the new life.

Paul had another kind of experience in Asia Minor. Timothy was with him. God never had to push Paul, he was on the go all the time. They tried to go into Asia, but "were forbidden by the Holy Spirit to speak the word" there. Then "they tried to enter Bithynia, but the Spirit of Jesus did not permit them," so they went on to Troas. This was the end of Asia Minor, and across the waters was Europe. During that night Paul had a vision: A Macedonian man stood and pleaded with him, "Cross over into Macedonia and help us." (This was no Freudian dream. When Paul got there it wasn't a man but a woman!) Here Luke had joined Paul. They *concluded* from the vision and the closed doors that God called them to go into Macedonia (Acts 16:6-10). Now they used the common process of thinking, putting together all they knew and then drawing an inference.

As Paul was making his last journey to Jerusalem he knew trouble lay ahead of him. But trouble, suffering, or persecution of any kind were never an argument for him against any course. He said at Miletus to the elders from Ephesus who came to bid him farewell, "I am bound by the Spirit to go to Jerusalem, and what is going to happen to me I do not know; except that the Holy Spirit in one city after another testifies to me that bonds and afflictions await me" (Acts 20:22-24). I have heard more than one Sunday school class decide that Paul should have turned back because trouble was ahead. But the fact that the Holy Spirit said there would be trouble did not mean to him that he was not to go. He added, "However, I am not concerned about anything; neither is my life dear to me except to finish my course and the ministry which I accepted from the Lord Jesus to bear witness to the gospel of the grace of God."

We may conclude that the way the communication comes is secondary. The most important fact is that communication from God is possible. The highest form of guidance is through our disciplined judgment enlightened by God's Word and directed by the Holy Spirit of God dwelling in the unconscious.

A recognition that guidance will always come, in time for any action, takes away the anxiety that closes the door between the conscious and the unconscious. This anxiety always hinders the work of God in our lives. It is not of faith. It breaks the release of power and communication.

Waiting is the hardest part of guidance for the western temperament. Several years ago Dr. Van Housen, the "Petticoat Surgeon" of Chicago, was being interviewed after her book had been reviewed. She was a woman of terrific action and courage. The interviewer asked her what her best advice, in one sentence, to others would be. Everyone was surprised. She said,

"Never make a decision until you have to." This would not be safe advice for a slothful person, but it is excellent for the person of action who finds it hard to wait. For those who wait on the Lord it could be said: Take everything into account, wait until the last minute for decision, and then use your judgment for the best decision possible.

Before the Second World War, in a discussion group in Chicago, a young man asked Douglas Steere how to act under his circumstances in relation to the war. He wanted to be told, but Dr. Steere was too wise for that. His answer was wisdom itself: "If on any issue I had only five per cent light and ninety-five per cent darkness, and had to make a decision, I would make the decision according to the five per cent light."

When I was a girl I used to ask my mother how I would know when the right man came along. She answered, "When you don't feel as though you have to ask someone else if he is the right man."

Last summer three-and-one-half-year-old Tommy came up to me and said, "Grandma, I love you." I answered, "Tommy, I love you, too." He said, "I know." I said, "How do you know I love you?" He thought deeply for a moment, then with a twinkle in his eye he said, "I just know." Perhaps, after all, the best guidance is like that. It can't be explained, we just *know*.

As we go on day by day in this fellowship with God, learning more about His way of living and doing things, we will be growing more like Him. We may accept for ourselves what Paul wrote to the Colossians (2:2), "We want you welded together in love and *moving on to all the riches that the full as-surance of insight brings with a knowledge of Christ, the mystery of God, in whom all the treasures of wisdom and knowledge lie hidden."

Jesus said, "If anyone wills to do His will he shall understand the teaching, whether it is from God or whether I speak from Myself" (John 7:17).

FOR FURTHER STUDY:

Read the fifth chapter of John very carefully.

Find how Jesus received guidance.

Find the hymns in your hymnbook under the subject of guidance. Compare with your experience.

List things you need guidance on.

What are you already sure of?

What do you feel uncertain about?

Do you have to have an answer now?

How is your waiting ability?

Have you learned to know the inner quietness where listening to God is possible?

God is faithful. Depend on Him.

Guidance is like an electronic-eye door. As you draw near the door will open.

Test it.

CHAPTER 17

Life Shared With God in Prayer

ALL KINDS OF PEOPLE PRAY. Some pray in emergencies only, others as a regular exercise of daily living. We must admit that prayer is good therapy. But we want to know if it is more than that.

The most wonderful thing about prayer is that the one who prays is always answered. Paul spoke out of his own experience while he was in jail for Christ's sake: "The Lord is near. Entertain no worry, but under all circumstances let your petitions be made known before God by prayer and pleading along with thanksgiving. So shall the peace of God, that surpasses all understanding, keep guard over your hearts and your thoughts in Christ Jesus" (Philippians 4:6,7).

If anxiety were conquered by prayer it would be a miracle in this fear-ridden world. What more can one ask?

Jesus says we can ask for more, for power to surpass His deeds! "The believer in Me shall do the deeds that I do, and shall do greater things than these, for I go to the Father, and I *will bring about whatever you ask in My name,* so that the Father may be glorified in the Son. *I will do whatever you ask in My name*" (John 14:12-14).

One of the greatest courses in prayer that one could take would be to take these words of Jesus as though He really meant them. We have to live in His Name before we are fully prepared to ask in His Name. We will let "our petitions be made known" as Paul suggested, and then as we become acclimated to the peace of God, we will grow in knowing how to pray in His Name. Then the petitioner is answered and so is

143

his petition. Of course, "no" is just as much of an answer as "yes," as any child knows.

Prayer must be taken seriously for it is dealing with power, the power of God. Too few take this power seriously. So the hungry people and the desperate people of the world turn to the big mail order business in prayer.

One of the first of such modern phenomena hit American headlines in 1929 with these words, "I talked with God — yes, I did — actually and literally." People were told that God-power was just waiting to be tapped; all that was necessary was to call on it with the spoken word, and all things would be possible. A set of lessons cost $28.00 or more, with money refunded if not helped. No one of the three million people in sixty-seven countries who took the lessons asked for any money back. In 1948 the "man who talked to God" died and it is not for us to say he is not continuing his conversation.

Should Jesus have offered a bargain, with money refunded, if not satisfied? Why are we so slow to listen to Him? Are we too often like the church at Sardis? "I know your doings, that you are said to live, but you are dead" (Revelation 3:1).

It seems almost useless to write more words when the book-case is already full of good books about prayer. Words! Words! That's our trouble. We talk *about* prayer and just don't pray. Or we say words aplenty, but we don't really pray.

The "Lord's Prayer" has suffered this fate through the centuries. This is ironical, because it was given in the first place to correct that lazy religious habit of merely saying words without really praying them.

The disciples were used to prayers that were *repeated*. They recognized something much different in the praying of Jesus. So one day they asked Him to teach them to pray (Luke 11: 1-4). Jesus gave them a prayer which is not only a prayer, but a pattern for prayer. If prayed sincerely it would bring about a real revolution, the kind that would set a mixed-up world in order.

Lord, teach us to pray.

Our Father: This prayer begins with a relationship. This is our relationship which is possible through the Holy Spirit of God.

The use of the word *Father* for God gives us the most authentic biography we have of Joseph as the earthly father of Jesus. He did not spoil the word for Jesus but gave it enough meaning so that Jesus, as an adult, could use the word for God, the heavenly Father.

There is one other thing we should note in the parent relationship. We parents know that when a little one comes up to us we are likely to ask, "What do you want?" It is a rebuke and an inspiration when the child answers, "I don't want anything, I just want to be with you."

Then we realize that the relationship is so much more important than mere giving or receiving things. The prayer of Jesus does not begin with asking for things. It begins with a relationship. This relationship in itself is a prayer.

Before this relationship is established, prayer is possible, but the prayer of the "outsider" is for reconciliation and for relationship. After we become children of God (He is our *Father*), we still fall short, but now the request is out of the faith of a child in the family asking for help in growth. And so the relationship grows as we become better acquainted with the Father.

It is *our* Father. We do not come alone, but with all the others whom the Father loves.

Who art in heaven: The Father God is near in relationship, but He is not a mere "father image." He is not mere god-quality in man. He is the Creator of the Universe. We might be afraid of Him if Jesus had not shown us He is love. To this all-powerful Creator we may come through the Spirit and say, "Our Father."

Hallowed be Thy name: The grandeur of the highest mountain, the beauty of the first daffodil in the spring, the bigness of the setting sun in midocean, the smile of a baby, or the Hallelujah Chorus are not symbol enough to express the hallowing of His Name by anyone who has known the unbelievable joy after empty years, of finding God as Father. The Jewish child's desire to bring honor to the family name becomes the spontaneous desire of the child of the heavenly Father, too.

The worship in this "Holy! Holy! Holy! art Thou" would ease the work of our church worship committees. They would no longer need to manipulate people's emotions to create worship atmosphere for our churches. In His Presence we worship spontaneously. "Thy name be held holy."

Thy kingdom come, Thy will be done on earth as it is in heaven: This is not an "otherworldly" prayer life. It isn't a prayer on a prayer wheel that we can set in motion while we go about our other duties. It is finding God's way in everything in our lives. This would revolutionize the church today, to say nothing of the world. This means all daily living is a prayer, not only what we say, but all we do.

Give us this day our daily bread: This sounds easy for we have food stocked up for weeks ahead. We pray this with relief until we note the "us." Then we have national embarrassment because of the food stored away in our country while people around the world starve. But we daren't vent ourselves on our government beyond where we have responsibility.

As we meditate on this in God's presence and as we pray it sincerely, the truth begins to sink in that we are *presenting ourselves* as God's stewards of *all* we possess and all we have responsibility for.

As a child I heard of a man baptized by immersion, who discovered as he came up out of the water that his wallet was still in his pocket. He said, "Oh, I did not intend to have my wallet baptized!" Wouldn't our finance boards have divine fun if church members really prayed this prayer?

Forgive us our debts as we forgive our debtors: In a day when guilt seems to be a universal "disease," we pray for forgiveness. The limitation in this prayer is an experience of healing. We are willing to face our own relationships and we ask not more than we give. However, as we have seen before, we could not ask for more. For unless we are ready to forgive others, we incapacitate ourselves to receive God's forgiveness. In God's presence we expose ourselves to His light and accept whatever He shows us. So we grow in love and that love is always a prayer.

Lead us not into temptation but deliver us from evil: This is the prayer Jesus Himself prayed for His disciples after His last supper with them and just before He was to be killed by the evil in men: "I do not pray that Thou wilt take them out of the world, but that Thou wilt preserve them from the evil one" (John 17:15). Jesus would not take His disciples out of the conflict with evil, but He would keep the evil out of them.

The pattern in temptation for the mature Christian is in Christ Himself: "For ours is not a High Priest who cannot sympathize with our weaknesses, but One who was in every respect tempted as we have been — but without sin. Let us then approach the throne of grace with assurance, so that we may receive mercy and find grace to help us in time of need" (Hebrews 4:15, 16).

For the mature Christian, as for Christ, the temptation was not in trifling with evil. It is hard to understand how a supposedly mature Christian can say, "I know what God wants me to do but I can't bring myself to do it" when the very beginning of this life in Christ is the complete commitment: "Thy will be done." Jesus never stumbled over "Will I do the Father's will or not?" That matter was settled for Him. He had only one question, "What is the Father's will?" That is the only question we dare have or can desire to have by the time we reach this part of the Lord's Prayer.

So the temptation is not to *do* evident evil. It is rather the danger of getting caught by beclouded evil. Temptation will likely come as it did for Jesus, "If you *are* the child of God." If it is a temptation related to the weaknesses of the old life, the appeal will come dressed up in clothes appropriate to the new life.

We will not go back to Jeremiah (17:9) for an alibi to cover our weakness: "The heart is deceitful above all things and utterly corrupt; who can know it?" Even Jeremiah was talking about the man who trusts in man and not in God, and he added that the "Lord searches the heart and tests the inner self." Paul assures us: "No temptation beyond human resistance has laid hold on you, and God is reliable, who will not permit you to be tempted beyond your ability, but will at the time of the temptation provide a way out, so that you will be able to stand it" (I Corinthians 10:13).

So *with faith* we pray, "Deliver us." This is important, for the first step off the road for the mature Christian is *anxiety.* No matter how hard it is to see the way in the fog which has come we are assured that in His faithfulness there is *a way out.* The only question, as we look to Him, is—what is His will for me at this time? Until that way is clear we *wait for* His revelation of the way out. The way may be dark but the waiting is alive with His presence. A friend on such a dark road wrote to me: "I am dependent upon Christ as never before. No bubbles now. Just a quiet, inner confidence in Him which is holding me steady beyond my belief in the midst of extreme pressures. I am seeing that God will move His purpose along and, instead of forcing ourselves into His purpose, we should just shout for joy that we can get into it. His will is no longer repulsive to me—it is exciting." We pray, "Lead us," because *we are following.*

Temptations which come are always matched to our years. In maturity they are not the same as to the "babe in Christ." For the Christian there can be no "old age" *complacency,* no heaviness of eye, no dullness of spirit. In Christ's presence there is never "old age," but a growing vibrancy of life.

There are other temptations of "experience" that we can watch for: We must guard against *cocksureness.* There is always a helplessness in human resources. Paul's "thorn in the flesh" helped him learn this. "He told me, 'My grace is sufficient for you, for My strength comes to perfection where there is weakness'" (II Corinthians 12:9). We are meant to live always in the power of God.

There is a coercive conservatism of "old age" which should never take hold of the mature Christian. This shows itself in the older Christian's temptation to impatience with others. It is hard to stay out of the "driver's seat," especially for the person of an aggressive disposition like Paul's. Waiting periods are good for this temptation.

Waiting before God is prayer indeed. And so we pray, "For Thine is the kingdom and the power and the glory." "Amen" is my personal signature to this wonderful prayer our Lord gave us.

In all the life of prayer we are cooperators with God. He is the main partner, we are only assistants, but we are assistants.

There is no need for anxiety even when we do not know how to pray: "The Spirit joins in to help us in our weakness; for we do not know what and how we ought to pray, but the Spirit Himself intercedes on our behalf with sighs too deep for words. And the Searcher of hearts knows what the Spirit has in mind, for He pleads with God on behalf of the saints" (Romans 8:26, 27).

Prayer is the greatest adventure in the world. It is cooperating with God in the use of His power.

ENTER THE SCHOOL OF PRAYER FOR FURTHER STUDY.

> Pray — Listen and talk to Him.
> Pray regularly whether you feel like it or not.
> List the things in you and your surroundings that are not according to the will of God and pray them into His will.
> One of the simplest and most helpful books is *Prayer — Conversing With God*, by Rosalind Rinker (Zondervan).

CHAPTER 18

Life Shared With Others

DURING THE SECOND WORLD WAR, I was on a Christian mission in one of the "concentration camps" we had for our Americans of Japanese ancestry. I lived with them behind barbed wire for ten days. I shall never forget their understanding, their lack of bitterness, their creative adjustment to financial loss and tragic social adjustment. Above all I shall never forget the pledge to the American flag I saw the high school students take.

Christian friendships made there carried over to the day when many of these wonderful people were settled in Chicago. One group of them shared space in a large city church until they bought an old church for themselves. This building had not been occupied for years. It needed everything done to it. They had little money, so they decided to do the repairs themselves.

The only man who had the experience to direct all this activity was seriously ill in the hospital. So they met to pray for his healing. He got well enough to be brought on a bed from the hospital each day to direct the work on the church. All who could, came in the daytime to work. Others came after daily jobs were finished, young people came after school, and all worked late into every night. Finally the church was in excellent condition.

The dedication day came. The director was now on his feet. For everyone it was a great day of restoration. My husband and I were there and we felt as though we were going through another Day of Pentecost. One of the young people said to the man who directed the work, "What will we do now, the work is finished?" He answered, "The work isn't finished, it is just ready to begin."

We need our buildings, but our beautiful church buildings are not *the church*. The church is *people, the fellowship of believers,* and we together are *the body of Christ* on earth.

"Conduct yourselves worthy of the calling you have received, with unalloyed humility and gentleness in a loving way patiently to bear with one another, making every effort to preserve the unity of the Spirit by the binding power of peace: one body and one Spirit, just as you received your calling, too, with one hope, one Lord, one faith, one baptism; one God and Father of all, who governs all and pervades all and is in us all.

"But to each individual of us the grace is granted and measured by the gift of Christ. . . . So has He given some to be evangelists, but others to be pastors and teachers, *to make the saints fit for the task of ministering toward the building up of the body of Christ, until we all* may arrive at the unity of faith and that understanding of the Son of God *that brings completeness of personality,* tending toward the measure of the stature of the fulness of Christ. As a result, we should *no longer be babes,* swung back and forth and carried around with every changing whiff of teaching that springs from human cunning and ingenuity for devising error; but lovingly attached to truth, *we should grow up in every way* toward Him who is the Head — Christ, out of whom the entire body is harmoniously fitted together and closely united by every contributing ligament, *with proportionate power for each single part to effect the development of the body for its upbuilding in love"* (Ephesians 4:1-16).

No Christian is alone in his relationship with God. He stands with all the others who love God. In fact, he has a real unity with these others, having the same Spirit and the same Lord.

In our era we rightly have a great interest in "groupness" and in "group dynamics." When the voice of fanaticism speaks for "groupness," the individual is sacrificed to the group. Those who fear this sacrifice, sacrifice the group for the individual. Only in Christ can we have a group (the church) in which what is good for the group is also good for the individual and what is good for the individual is good for the group.

When groupness is an end in itself, it is plagued by mediocrity in the name of unity. The Holy Spirit is the great individualizer and at the same time we are brought together in a unity in Him. We do not have to contrive this unity, we join it.

The purpose of the fellowship in the body of Christ is mutual growth: "Until *we* all arrive — into completeness of personality." The second purpose of this fellowship is to represent Christ in the world. We are His body. "On behalf of Christ, then, we are ambassadors, God as it were making the appeal through us" (II Corinthians 5:20).

My precious friend, Rosa Page Welch, was given a new name when she sang to the Christians of her own race in Africa: Mama B'lambwa NSango, which means, "Pick up the Good News she has brought."

And so the blinding veil vanishes!

"As with unveiled face we see the Lord's glory mirrored, we are changed into the same likeness, from one degree of glory to another, derived as it is from the Lord's Spirit."

Do not be afraid. *Say 'Yes' to Life.*

FOR FURTHER STUDY:

Read I Corinthians 12 and list the characteristics there of the fellowship of believers.

If you have no prayer group in your church, find some believers who pray (Matthew 18:19, 20). Together consider the strength of your church and praise God. Then list the problems in one column and in another God's will on these issues. Then pray until the first column is lost in the second. When that happens you will know much about the power of God available to us on earth, and about the fellowship of believers.

THE ZONDERVAN PAPERBACK SERIES

THE POWER OF POSITIVE PRAYING — John Bisagno   No. 9238s
THE REBELLIOUS PLANET — Lon Woodrum   No. 12292s
YOU CAN WITNESS WITH CONFIDENCE — Rosalind Rinker
   No. 10714s
APOSTLE TO THE ILLITERATES (Frank C. Laubach)—David Mason
   No. 10141s
THE GOSPEL BLIMP — Joe Bayly   No. 12288s
FREEDOM FROM THE SEVEN DEADLY SINS — Billy Graham
   No. 9716s

96 pages each, 69c

A BIT OF HONEY (After-dinner speeches) — W. E. Thorn
   No. 10928s
PLAY BALL! — James Hefley   No. 9797s
PRAYER — CONVERSING WITH GOD — Rosaline Rinker
   No. 10716s
HOW TO ENJOY THE CHRISTIAN LIFE—Don Mainprize   No. 10106s
THESE MY PEOPLE — Lillian Dickson   No. 9524s
LIFE IS FOR LIVING — Betty Carlson   No. 9384s
SCIENCE RETURNS TO GOD — James H. Jauncey   No. 9927s
NEVER A DULL MOMENT — Eugenia Price   No. 10584s
THE BIBLE FOR TODAY'S WORLD — W. A. Criswell   No. 9426s

128 pages each, 79c

ABOVE OURSELVES — James H. Jauncey   No. 9950s
BECOMING A CHRISTIAN — Rosalind Rinker   No. 10718s
BUT GOD! — V. Raymond Edman   No. 9595s
FIND OUT FOR YOURSELF — Eugenia Price   No. 10603s
LIVING CAN BE EXCITING — Aaron N. Meckel   No. 12280s
THE SAVING LIFE OF CHRIST — W. Ian Thomas   No. 10980s
YOUR CHILD — Anna B. Mow   No. 12256s
SAY 'YES' TO LIFE — Anna B. Mow   No. 10383s
KNOWING GOD'S SECRETS — John Hunter   No. 9883s
THEY FOUND THE SECRET — V. Raymond Edman   No. 9564s
WE'RE NEVER ALONE — Eileen Guder   No. 9710s
MAN TO MAN — Richard C. Halverson   No. 6818s

160 pages each, 89c

A WOMAN'S WORLD — Clyde Narramore   No. 12230s
HELLBENT FOR ELECTION — P. Speshock   No. 10830s
LIFE AND LOVE — Clyde Narramore   No. 10412s
YOUNG ONLY ONCE — Clyde Narramore   No. 10414s
HOW TO WIN OVER WORRY — John Haggai   No. 9740s

192 pages each, 98c

WOMAN TO WOMAN — Eugenia Price   No. 10589s
PILGRIM'S PROGRESS — John Bunyan   No. 6610s
LET MY HEART BE BROKEN — Richard Gehman   No. 9694s

Approximately 256 pages each, 98c